A Joy
I'd Never
Known

When I Gave Up Control, I Found . . .

A Joy
I'd Never
Known

JAN DRAVECKY

with Connie Neal

ZondervanPublishingHouse

Grand Rapids, Michigan

A Division of HarperCollinsPublishers

96 97 98 99 00 01 02 /❖ DH/ 10 9 8 7 6 5 4 3 2 1

To my Tiffany,
May you always know the joy I'd never known.

Contents

Acknowledgments

I truly celebrate the completion and publication of this book. My deep appreciation goes to many people who have participated in making my dream a reality.

To Connie Neal—who contributed her creative and writing gifts to this book and labored with me to put my story on paper. She shared my passion and desire to see that my story was shared so that others may know they are not alone. I love you, sister.

To my editors, Sandy Vander Zicht and Lori Walburg—who did such an excellent job of molding and shaping this book. Thank you so much for your hard work, expertise, and patience with me!

To my friend Carla Muir—thank you for lending your incredible talents, poetry, and insight to this book. I treasure your listening ear, your wit, and most importantly, your friendship.

To my agents, Sealy and Susan Yates—who have always been there to guide and counsel. You are dear to my heart, always.

To my publisher, Zondervan—thank you for your belief in this book and for your genuine care and concern for Dave and me that went beyond business.

To my husband, David—whose unbelivable heart for God, the Truth, and others inspired me to write this book. I appreciate your encouragement and constant support so much. You always believed I could do it. I praise God for your love and commitment to me always. I love you.

To my children, Tiffany and Jonathan—thank you for giving Mom the time I needed to see this to completion. I just love you so much!

To my Heavenly Father—thank you for the Truth of your Word. Thank you for loving me enough to not let me stay the way I was. Thank you for never letting go of me. May the glory be to you.

Chronology
of Events

March 31, 1956. Janice Roh is born in Youngstown, Ohio.

May 26, 1972. At age sixteen, Jan has her first date with Dave Dravecky.

June 1978. Dave is drafted by the Pittsburgh Pirates.

October 7, 1978. Jan marries Dave Dravecky.

October 1979. The Draveckys move to Barranquilla, Columbia, for winter ball, and Jan loses her faith in a loving God.

September 1980. The Draveckys move to Florida with plans to set up a permanent home there. Jan works full time at a C.P.A. firm.

April 1981. Dave is traded to the San Diego Padres and sent to Amarillo, Texas. Jan stays in Florida to work.

August 27, 1981. Dave and Jan profess faith in Jesus Christ and are baptized together.

April 1982. Dave is promoted to Triple-A ball, and they move to Honolulu, Hawaii.

June 6, 1982. Tiffany Dravecky is born in Honolulu.

June 8, 1982. Dave is called up to the major leagues by the San Diego Padres.

June 12, 1982. Jan moves to San Diego with Tiffany while Dave is on the road.

July 4, 1982. Jan and Tiffany fly to Ohio to visit Jan's parents.

July 31, 1982. Jan's mother dies suddenly of a heart attack while watching Dave pitch his first major league game.

August 1982. Jan flies to Ohio for her mom's funeral. Stays three weeks to take care of father and brother.

April 1983. The Draveckys move to San Diego, where they live until 1987.

July 6, 1983. Dave is chosen to represent the National League in the All-Star game.

October 1984. Dave plays in the World Series for the San Diego Padres.

January 8, 1985. Jonathan Dravecky is born in San Diego.

July 4, 1987. Dave is traded to San Francisco Giants.

October 7, 1987. Ninth wedding anniversary. Dave pitches in the championship series and wins 5–0.

January 26, 1988. Dave has MRI test on his left arm; the results are inconclusive.

April 4, 1988. Dave pitches opening day against the Los Angeles Dodgers in Dodger Stadium, winning 5–1.

August 1988. Draveckys move back to Ohio.

September 19, 1988. Second MRI test on Dave's arm indicates there is a tumor, and a biopsy is needed.

October 7, 1988. Tenth wedding anniversary. Dave undergoes surgery to remove the tumor and one half of the deltoid muscle in his left arm. To kill all cancerous cells, part of his humerus bone is frozen. Dr. Muschler tells Jan, "Apart from a miracle, Dave will never pitch again."

November 15, 1988. Dave shows Jan he can go through his pitching motions. Jan supports Dave's efforts to recover and pitch again.

April 1989. Draveckys move back to San Francisco from Ohio.

July 23, 1989. Dave pitches his first complete game for the Class-A San Jose Giants in Stockton, California, before 4,200 fans and wins 2–0.

August 10, 1989. Dave pitches again in a major league game at Candlestick Park in what becomes known as his comeback game. Media blitz begins. Mail starts pouring in.

August 15, 1989. While Dave is pitching in Montreal and Jan is listening to the game on radio in San Francisco, Dave's humerus bone snaps. Dave and Jan simultaneously have a sense of supernatural peace that becomes their "vision" that God is doing something bigger than baseball. Media blitz intensifies.

September 5, 1989. Jan receives call in San Francisco that her father has died.

October 9, 1989. Dave breaks his arm a second time while celebrating victory of the San Francisco Giants in the National League playoffs.

October 17, 1989. Press conference to announce signing of contract for Dave's book *Comeback*. An earthquake interrupts the World Series.

October 25, 1989. Jan decides to move the family back to Ohio.

October 27, 1989. Doctors at Cleveland Clinic say that the tumor has returned.

November 1, 1989. Draveckys invite Kristen to live with their family so Jan can help her.

November 13, 1989. Dave announces retirement from baseball.

January 4, 1990. Dave has surgery to perform radiation therapy, remove tricep, and remaining part of the deltoid muscle.

March 21, 1990. Jan experiences first panic attack in J. W. Marriott hotel, Washington, D.C.

March 22, 1990. Dravecky family meets President George Bush at the White House when Dave is honored with Award of Courage by American Cancer Society.

March 1990. *Comeback* published. Dave and Jan start book tour, making some appearances together.

April 6, 1990. Dave and Jan fly to New York to appear on *Good Morning, America.* While at CBS studios, Jan collapses and has to return home to Ohio. Dave continues on book tour.

April 10, 1990. Jan is sent to a psychiatrist and is diagnosed with clinical depression. Dave cancels book tour and returns home.

April 15, 1990. Jan goes to a Christian counselor and is diagnosed with depression.

April 30, 1990. Jan decides to stop seeing counselor.

May 1, 1990. Jan decides to try complete bed rest to recover from exhaustion.

May 7, 1990. Dave undergoes third surgery and is told he may lose his arm.

Summer 1990. Dave endures eight weeks of radiation therapy to kill cancer in his arm.

July 17, 1990. Dave and Jan tape segment for Billy Graham Evangelistic Crusade.

August 9, 1990. Jan diagnosed by medical doctor Dr. McGowen as having depression and goes on Prozac medication.

August 9, 1990. Jan seeks help from pastor.

August 16, 1990. Jan still too weak to even go to the pool with Dave and her children. Shakes her fist at God and tries to walk away.

September 23, 1990. Dave and Jan go on retreat with staff of Focus on the Family.

September 30, 1990. Dave is hospitalized with severe staph infection for five days.

November 1990. Jan starts to feel the depression lifting and decides to have doctor wean her off Prozac.

February 1991. Symptoms of depression return, but Dave is now convinced Jan doesn't need professional help.

May 1991. Jan asks Dave to let her go into inpatient treatment for depression. Dave ends conversation by breaking the phone.

May 19, 1991. Dave and Jan go to California to tape Focus on the Family radio broadcast. Sealy Yates recommends book by Dr. Henry Cloud and arranges meeting with Dr. John Townsend.

May 23, 1991. Dave and Jan begin counseling with Dr. Loren Sommers in Ohio.

June 7, 1991. Dave calls Jan from New York to tell her the doctors say it's time to amputate his arm.

June 18, 1991. Dave goes in for cancer surgery. His left arm and shoulder are amputated.

September 1991. Draveckys start writing *When You Can't Come Back*.

October 1991. Barbara Walters interview airs on *20/20*.

July 1993. Draveckys move to Colorado and open offices for Outreach of Hope.

Summer 1995. Jan realizes God's promise of joy.

Introduction

*A*t the prime age of thirty-four, my life took a detour—not one I had planned. My journey took me into the valley of panic attacks, anxiety, and depression. I had never known anyone who had ever experienced something like this, and as a committed Christian for over eight years, I did not understand how this could be happening to me. I wondered what was wrong with me. Guilt engulfed me. I felt alone, confused, and scared.

Turning to the Christian world around me for direction, I found them to be just as ignorant as I was. I felt their judgment as I sank deeper and deeper into depression. I needed a lifeline. I needed to know there was a way out of the dark hole I was in. I needed to be shown the way up and out.

God did throw me that lifeline, pulling me out of the dark hole and into his light. Teaching me to let go, molding and shaping me with his truth, he brought healing into my life. At one point I believed I would never feel joy again, but in time he taught me a joy I'd never known.

I am sharing my journey so honestly in this book to give hope to others who are going through the same valley of depression. God tells us that we are to comfort others as he has comforted us (2 Corinthians 1:3–5). If you are going through depression or another valley of adversity, be comforted in knowing that you are not alone in your journey. God is faithful to his promises.

Join me on my journey through the valley, but do not get discouraged along the way. Although the journey will seem quite dark and stormy at times, a beautiful rainbow awaits us at the end.

A Journey Not My Own

As a youth with plans and dreams
I set my course ahead.
I owned the world and all its worth.
Not following—I led.

I often sought new travelers
and helped them find their way.
So strong was I, they did not know
my vessel was of clay.

Not one was more prepared than I
for raging storms at sea.
But I ignored small leaks and cracks
within that vessel—me.

I drifted in deep waters far
away from those I love,
Convinced that I was all alone
and God somewhere above.

And in the darkness of my sea
I heard a soft voice say,
"I'm by your side to mend your ship,
my precious one of clay."

It's then that I had realized
though God was at my side,
I was the one who set the course
with all my senseless pride.

I now have found an inner peace—
my journey's not my own.
With Jesus at the helm I have
a joy I'd never known.

Carla Muir

One

Panic Attack!

*T*he doorman nodded as my husband, Dave, and I walked through the enormous doors of the J. W. Marriott Hotel next door to the White House. It was March 21, 1990. Our family had been invited to the White House to meet President Bush, who would present Dave with an Award of Courage from the American Cancer Society.

Seven-year-old Tiffany and five-year-old Jonathan looked about the room with awe. Grand crystal chandeliers adorned the ceiling of the spacious lobby. The pale colors, fine furnishings, and marble pillars added to the sense of traditional beauty, and everyone in the room seemed to take on greater dignity by virtue of the impressive surroundings. As we approached the front desk, Dave talked with the president of the American Cancer Society while I stood next to them, chatting with our escort from the White House.

Suddenly, out of nowhere, fear grabbed me by the throat. One moment I was chatting politely; the next moment the room began to sway. I couldn't catch my breath; I was dizzy. My heart pounded in my chest, harder and harder, faster and faster. *Oh, God,* I thought, clutching at Dave's sleeve, *is this what it feels like to die?*

"David." I tugged more insistently, my throat tight with fear. "David, I can't breathe."

Finally he turned to me, a bit of irritation in his eyes. "Jan, what's wrong?"

I couldn't even tell him. The room spun around me, and my heart felt like it was about to explode. *I have to get out of here!* I thought.

Grabbing the children by the hand, I ran outside, gulping for air. *Breathe, Jan, just breathe!* Flinging my head back, I inhaled deeply as Tiffany and Jonathan watched, puzzled and curious.

Then Dave was beside me. I clutched him. "David, pray for me," I gasped. "Something is wrong."

He took my arm and reassured me. "Jan, you're fine. You're fine! What's wrong with you?"

"I can't breathe."

"What do you mean you can't breathe?" The puzzled look on his face deepened.

"I don't know," I wailed. "I'm just so afraid!"

His eyes flashed with impatience and disbelief—and I could understand why. This was not like me. As long as Dave had known me, I had always been a picture of perfect control. So why was I making such a scene in front of all these bigwigs?

In Dave's steadying presence, my dizziness and shortness of breath subsided. "I'm fine now," I said, smiling weakly.

"We need to get back to our hosts," Dave said, quietly but firmly. "Just stay calm till we get to our room."

I nodded. Still taking deep breaths, I allowed him to lead me through the double doors and back into the lobby.

Our host and the rest of our group greeted us with polite smiles when we rejoined them outside the elevator. Dave held me firmly with a gaze that was both a strength and a warning. But when I saw the doors of the elevator open and imagined going inside, fear struck me once again.

"David, I can't get in the elevator," I whispered desperately.

"Of course you can!" he whispered back.

I got in the elevator, but fear got in with me. When the doors closed, I was trapped. My thoughts raced back and forth between the certainty that I was about to die and questions about my sanity. Trying to control my terrifying thoughts and feelings, I fixed my eyes on the numbers lighting up as we passed each floor. *Am I going crazy?* I thought. *Is this a nervous breakdown? No! This can't be happening to me. Oh, God, how can this be happening to me?*

My terror was so complete that when the doors finally opened to release me, I was grateful to still be alive.

Dave led the children and me into our room, an unbelievably gorgeous suite. But I couldn't enjoy my surroundings. I could barely stand up. Lying on the bed, I cried while my mind raced, seeking a reason for this awful feeling.

Dave and I were getting ready for a week of important appearances to promote *Comeback*, a book Dave had written in which our Christian faith played a major role. In our visits to *Entertainment Tonight, Good Morning America, CBS This Morning*, and other major network programs, we hoped to share our faith in front of the American public.

Suddenly it dawned on me. Maybe I was under spiritual attack! Maybe Satan wanted to keep us from speaking publicly.

"David, come pray for me," I begged. "I'm under attack."

Dave prayed over me, but nothing happened.

My thoughts raced on. Could it be a heart attack? After all, heart disease ran in my family. Or maybe my panic was the result of my low blood sugar. But I'd never heard of anyone dying from that condition—and I felt dangerously close to death.

A thought nagged at me from the back of my mind. Could this be what my sister-in-law, Missy, had described to me a month before? She'd gone through what she called a panic attack, and it had been the first loose thread in her unraveling mental health. Missy used to be just like me: fun, strong-willed, extremely capable, with an aggressive love of life. Then she started having panic attacks that took such control of her that she couldn't even drive a car. She grew more and more apprehensive. Only a short time later, Missy entered the hospital for psychiatric treatment.

Could this be a panic attack? I quickly dismissed the thought.

The thought of being mentally unstable scared me—not like the panic that gripped me now and threatened my life, but in another way. Mental illness happened to other people, weak people. *I* wasn't weak; in fact, my mind was my greatest strength. *No*, I told myself, *that could never happen to me*. I determined that this was not a psychological problem, as though my determination made it so.

I lay in the bed, waiting for my body to obey my mental commands, which told the terrible feelings to go away. But they didn't. I lay there still crying, still fearful.

There are moments when, looking back, you realize your life has taken a new course. That moment, lying in bed in the J. W. Marriott, was such a moment. As I reconsider what led me to that moment and retrace the steps I have taken since then, I begin to understand why God did not let my life go the way I had wanted it to go.

From that moment, God took my life on another route, on a journey I would not have chosen for myself, one that went though a dark and frightening valley. Along the way I learned valuable lessons I could not have learned by staying on the high road where the sun is always shining.

I thought I had lost my way. Actually, I *did* lose *my* way—in order to follow *God's* way. Just because *I* didn't know where I was going or where I would arrive, my journey wasn't uncharted.

It was simply a journey not my own.

Two

Mother's Strong Little Girl

*E*ven as a child, I loved to plan my life. Having a route to follow gave me a sense of security, and I hated any surprise or detour in my predetermined path. When I read a book, I always read the last page first to make sure I knew what to expect. When I watched a movie, I drove my mother crazy, always wanting to know what was going to happen next so that nothing would catch me off guard.

My mother made sure I had a protected childhood. She wouldn't let me watch anything sad because I would be disturbed for days afterward. She kept me safe from all the pain and unpleasantness of life, and while that may have helped the child, it definitely did not prepare me for the life that was to come.

I came from a two-parent family in which Mom and Dad loved each other and loved me. The older of two children, I was an extremely self-assured child and had no problems achieving whatever I set my mind to do. Mother never worried about me because life seemed to come easy for me. I had always been her strong little girl.

I had definite plans for my life. I dreamed I'd become a successful career woman, marry a professional, live in our hometown of Boardman, Ohio, have two children—a boy and a girl—and live happily ever after. Only one part of this story wasn't like a fairy tale; I wasn't expecting some Prince Charming to do this for me. I planned to make this happen for myself.

At age sixteen, I dated a guy who introduced me to his friend Dave. Shortly after I met Dave, his friend broke up with me, and I was brokenhearted. I was done with men forever. They caused pain, and I wanted to avoid pain at all costs. But as soon as Dave knew I had broken up with his friend, he started calling me, hounding me to go out with him. I told him, "Thanks, but no thanks!" I was not interested.

Dave continued to call despite my rejection. My mother had always liked Dave. She knew he had something special that made him stand out from all the others. When she brought this to my attention, I had to agree. He seemed very aggressive and always got what he went after; but he had a gentle, tender side that attracted me. He was truly a cut above all the other boys I knew.

After much persistence on Dave's part, I finally agreed to go out with him for the first time on May 26, 1972. After that first date, Dave told me he would marry me someday. I thought, *Oh my! You are totally crazy!* I ran home to my mother and exclaimed, "Mother, Mother, he said he wants to marry me!"

She kindly and wisely advised, "Jan, just because you went out on a date with him does not mean you are going to marry him. Just give him time."

She calmed me down and encouraged me to continue dating Dave. So he and I continued to see each other throughout our junior and senior years of high school. We broke up a few times in college, but in our junior year, we finally got engaged.

I was an accounting major, which suited me perfectly. I loved learning how to make everything balance, keeping all my ducks in a row, planning and organizing. I liked predicting outcomes, and I found comfort in the dependable patterns of mathematics. In addition to attending college in the evenings, I worked full time as a bookkeeper for a construction company during the day. It was a demanding schedule, but I loved it.

Dave went to the same community college during the day. His major was definitely baseball. He made it through his first two years by enrolling in courses he could pass without attending class. Talk about opposites attracting! During his junior year—when we got engaged—he became more serious about his studies, attending classes and getting A's and B's.

Dave did exceptionally well playing college baseball, but I wasn't enamored with the prestige that could come with being married to a professional baseball player. Rather, I saw the disadvantages of the baseball lifestyle. Moving from town to town was not my idea of a secure life. Far from it!

While everyone else was praying and hoping Dave would be drafted into professional baseball, I was secretly praying he wouldn't. I didn't want him to chase rainbows. I wanted him to choose a career he could count on. Much to my dismay, however, Dave was drafted by the Pittsburgh Pirates during our senior year of college and sent to the minor leagues. I had the entire summer to adjust my plans and accept that baseball was going to be our way of life.

Dave and I were married on October 7, 1978, after his first summer in the minors. And I went from being mother's strong little girl to being a strong woman, perfectly suited for life in professional baseball. Dave and I lived baseball. We were in this together; he was out there on the field, but he relied on my support to enable him to play the game he loved. Minor league baseball players don't make much money. Dave's starting salary was $500 a month, and each year, it went up in increments of only $50 per month. So my salary as an accountant supported us. During tax season, I worked between sixty and ninety hours per week to pay our bills during the summer. We used to count pennies so I could cash them in to get quarters for the laundry. Yet those were the best times.

From 1978 to 1981, we were on the move, going wherever the team sent Dave. We lived in Buffalo, New York; Sarasota, Florida; Barranquilla, Columbia; Ohio; New York (again); Florida (again); Amarillo, Texas; Puerto Rico; and back to Ohio. I became proficient at packing and moving, although my dream had always been to settle down.

To my surprise, I really enjoyed the baseball life. I thought God had put me in this situation because I was so well-suited for it. I was self-sufficient, able to live my life alone, and that's exactly what I had to do. Although it was a rather lonely life, I felt uniquely prepared to handle it, and I commended myself for this.

Baseball is not like football, where players are drafted immediately into the professional ranks. In baseball, players are first drafted into the minor leagues. Then it's rather like climbing a ladder. There's "Rookie," "A," "Double-A," "Triple-A," and then finally the major leagues. Players can skip rungs on the ladder, but for the most part, they put in their time at each rung in hopes of eventually making it to the majors. Only two percent make it to the big leagues, while most players spend their time going up and down the ladder.

A special camaraderie exists among ballplayers and their wives in the minor leagues. Our best year in the minors was 1981 in Double-A ball in Amarillo, Texas. A large group of us had all become Christians together that summer, and Dave and I were baptized on August 27, 1981. In April of 1982, we and our Christian friends were all promoted to Triple-A together. It was such an exciting time!

We all moved to Hawaii for Triple-A, and our sense of expectancy was tangible—we were just one phone call away from the major leagues. But we were expectant in another way as well. There were eight pregnant wives on the team, and I was among them. I was due to deliver in June of 1982.

Three

You Can Handle It!

*B*eing nine months pregnant in the summertime is uncomfortable, even in exotic Hawaii. There's always a wonderful breeze, but the breeze is hot, not mild and balmy. The guys had been gone on a road trip for several weeks, leaving the eight of us waddling around our high-rise apartments, waiting for nature to take its course.

I wanted my mother to be with me for the birth of my baby, but she was in Ohio and afraid to fly across the ocean. When I called her, she said, "Jan, you'll handle it just fine, the way you handle everything else." She never talked to me about childbirth, of what I might expect. Instead, she avoided discussing it, just as she avoided other painful realities of life.

Friday night, June 4, 1982, I saw a show of blood and called my friend Jackie in a mild panic.

"Jackie, I think I lost my mucous plug." We'd learned all about this in our childbirth classes, but it was quite different to realize this momentous event was beginning to happen. "What do I do?"

"Call the doctor. You'd better call Dave in Phoenix, too."

Dave wasn't due home for a week, but I called him and told him to come home. He wanted me to talk to the doctor and make sure. When I called Dr. Nakasoni, he seemed unreasonably calm. He questioned me carefully, told me to call him if I started having consistent pains, and suggested I stop by, tomorrow.

Stop by, tomorrow? What was he thinking?

I was thinking, *I don't want to go into labor all alone!* I wanted Dave or my mom with me. No matter how strong I appeared on the outside, inside I was a frightened young woman.

My friend Jackie Hawkins had given birth two months before. She volunteered to sleep over with me in case anything happened. Jackie, her baby, and I shared our king-sized bed that night. Sleeping was hard when I feared that every minor cramp heralded the onset of labor. For all I knew, the rhythmic tightening of my belly might be my only preparation for releasing this baby. I did sleep some, but not well.

Saturday morning Jackie drove me to the doctor's office in the car we affectionately called "Martha." Several of us couples were so poor that we had pooled $750 to buy the car, a lime green Duster without air conditioning that belched fumes that left us coughing. I emerged from the Duster, feeling such expectancy I could barely contain myself.

Please, say I'm in labor! I mentally begged the doctor as he examined me. If he said the word, Dave would be on the next plane out of Phoenix. And soon we would be parents!

The doctor examined me and pronounced that my cervix was completely closed. I was terribly let down. I wanted to have the baby now!

To soothe my disappointment we decided to eat out, treating ourselves to French toast at King's Bakery. Then I called David and told him it was a false alarm.

The rest of the day I hung around with the other wives. When our husbands were away, living in the apartment building was like living in a college dorm as we visited back and forth from apartment to apartment. Around 9:00 P.M. I told my friends, "I'm beat. I think I'll go upstairs and try to get some sleep." After the doctor's discouraging exam, I figured I would carry the baby at least another two weeks.

I fell into an exhausted sleep. At 1:00 A.M. I woke up, and I was completely wet. *What am I going to do?* I thought. *I can't call anyone and wake them up again. What if it's another false alarm?* Since it was 7:00 A.M. in Ohio, I called my mom.

"Mom, I think my water broke, and I'm all alone. I don't know what to do."

"Honey, what can I do? I'm in Ohio."

She encouraged me to call one of my friends there in the apartments. Even though I didn't want to inconvenience anyone by awakening her in the middle of the night, I finally convinced myself that this probably was the real thing, so I apologetically called my friend Katie, who was eight months pregnant. She urged me to call Dr. Nakasoni, then proceeded to wake up five other friends.

Dr. Nakasoni confirmed that my water had broken and told me to go straight to the hospital. By this time, my apartment bustled with six friends, so I had one of my other friends call Dave and tell him to come home immediately.

I was so excited that I was going to get to see Dave, I didn't go straight to the hospital. I got in the shower, planning to wash and set my hair so I would look nice for Dave. (My mother's protective silence about childbirth had left me so naive!)

I was in the shower when the first real contraction hit. This was the one that made me understand the knowing smile on Dr. Nakasoni's face when I described the previous warm-up contractions as though they were the real thing. I screamed, which made my friends come running. They started scurrying around in a frenzy, trying to get everything ready for me to go to the hospital. I insisted on setting my hair while they timed my contractions, which were coming regularly two minutes apart.

What a sight we were: a group of frantic women, three of us pregnant, one still in rollers, piling into our lime green "Martha." Without the protection of decent shock absorbers, I felt every bump severely, especially those we hit while I was in the middle of a contraction. Still, I tried to put the finishing touches on my makeup at stoplights. My friends laughed from nervousness as much as genuine amusement as I took out the last of my rollers and tried to brush my hair while we bounced along toward the hospital in the middle of the night.

At the hospital, they checked me and found that I had dilated only one centimeter. That was fine with me. Now I wanted this process to slow down enough so that Dave would have time to fly across the ocean to be with me for the birth. My six friends took turns staying with me as I labored through the night, my contractions still two minutes apart. No one said anything, but I knew they all silently hoped Dave would get there in time for the birth. I recall thinking at some point in the process, *Well, I guess I have to do this on my own, too.* But labor doesn't give one time for much contemplation. That point passed, and I focused completely on just getting through each contraction.

When I was dilated to only eight-and-a-half centimeters I had an involuntary reflex to push. But if I gave in to this impulse before I was fully dilated, I would rip myself terribly. The hospital staff offered me medication, but I remained determined to complete the birth naturally. When I began pushing prematurely, my friend Katie jumped up on the bed, grabbed my face, and breathed with me the way we'd been taught in our childbirth class. "Blow, blow, blow, blow!" she commanded. As drastic as that was, she helped me focus enough to resist the overpowering urge to push until my body was ready.

Morning dawned. I continued to pant and blow, holding back, hoping Dave would arrive before the birth.

Around 11:00 A.M., someone left to get Dave from the airport. By this point, I barely noticed. The young woman who had insisted on rolling her hair to look pretty for her husband had become a woman with no concern for appearances. Real life has a way of putting appearances in perspective. They wheeled me down the hospital corridor toward delivery with my legs in stirrups and the baby's head crowning. Modesty was a thing of the past.

They kept telling me to look in the mirror so I could see the baby's head, but I didn't want to look. We made it to the delivery room, where I saw Dr. Nakasoni. He was still wearing khaki shorts and thong sandals, apparently having been called off the golf course for the delivery. My friends were all around me, excitedly telling me, "Look, look in the mirror. You can see his head. Look, here comes Joshua." (We were sure it would be a boy.) I didn't want to look. I just wanted this baby out of me.

I was pushing in earnest now. I could do this on my own. I was strong enough.

"You're doing great, Jan."

"He's almost here. Just one more push. That's good."

He turned out to be a she. Tiffany Marie Dravecky was born at 11:39 A.M., June 6, 1982. The nurse cleaned and wrapped her, then placed her in my arms. I held her close, still dazed by the ordeal. Then she opened these luminous blue eyes and looked at me for the first time.

"Oh, my—she's got her father's eyes," I breathed. This new little person, this little girl, was looking at me, wide-eyed.

"Hi, I'm your mommie," I said to her, touching her face lightly with my fingers, marveling at her tiny nose and tiny ears.

I held her for only a few minutes before they took her away. It had been a rough birth, but even with the pain, I felt a deep sense of satisfaction.

About an hour and a half later, Dave bounded through the door. He took one look at me and shuddered. "Whoa! You must have had it rough."

"Yes, I did. I certainly did."

What a humbling moment. My lips were parched and cracked. My face was swollen, and it bore the marks of Katie's hands. My hair had lost all memory of its curls. Dave was happy to see me, but he was more eager to see Tiffany. I can't say I blame him. Even as crinkled as she was, she must have looked better than I did.

By the second day after her birth, I started to feel better. Dave brought me a bouquet of miniature, pale peach tea roses. His parents sent a bouquet of big red anthirium. The flowers in the room and the beautiful blue Hawaiian skies beyond my window reminded me of the wonder and beauty that were temporarily lost in the pain of childbirth. Now that I had accomplished "having a baby," the thought of loving and caring for her appealed to me. I was even starting to feel pretty again.

On the third day, the day I was to go home, I hobbled painfully toward the bathroom to put on my makeup before Dave arrived. As I carefully applied mascara and blush, I looked forward to the weeks ahead. Dave would be home for twenty-one days, and we would have time together to bond with Tiffany. Secretly, I also looked forward to having someone pamper me too. It was hard for me to let anyone know my needs, but I actually looked forward to letting Dave take care of me for a while.

When the phone rang, I eased myself to the edge of the bed. It was Dave.

"Jan, you're not going to believe this." His voice was tinged with a strange excitement. "I got the call. I got called up to the major leagues."

"What?"

I began crying hysterically. My nurse and roommate thought I'd received news that someone had died. But all that had died were my dreams. My plan to be pampered. My twenty-one days with Dave and the baby.

He's going to leave me all alone with this baby, I thought. *I can't believe it. Will someone ever take care of me? I'm always there for them. Who will ever be there for me?*

I didn't dare express these feelings out loud. They seemed too selfish and ungrateful. How could I complain to my friends who lived for the day that their husbands would get the call to the major leagues? How could I begrudge Dave the fulfillment of his life's dream?

They wanted Dave to come to San Diego immediately before I even came home from the hospital. Dave called them back and asked if he could have an extra day. "My wife has just given birth to our first child," he explained.

"Look," they said, "if you're not there to fill the spot at the appointed time, someone else will be."

So Dave brought me home Tuesday afternoon, and we shared one night together as a new family before Dave left for San Diego the next day. Tiffany and I were left alone.

On Thursday, the other guys came back home to their wives, so I didn't even have the support of my friends to lean on. After all, I didn't want to get in the way of their reunions.

Over the next several days, I had bouts of self-pity, but I consoled myself with the thought that I always had enjoyed a new challenge. I had to start packing and getting ready for the move to San Diego.

Everything we owned fit into two trunks. One trunk held a set of avocado-green dishes, sheets, towels, pots, and pans. My spices also went into that trunk because they were too expensive to replace every time we moved. The other trunk held my clothes and what few baby things I had for Tiffany. We were so sure we were going to have a boy that most of our gifts weren't appropriate for a little girl, so I gave the boy clothes to my friends who were still expecting.

Meanwhile, I was having a hard time adjusting to motherhood. Tiffany kept me up all night, and my body was still adjusting to nursing and tremendous hormonal changes. I knew these took place after having a baby, but the constant discomfort grated on me and wore away at my usually sunny disposition. As I resigned myself to the situation, a sadness and loneliness I had never known before settled into my soul.

Our friends were in and out, helping me get my things together and offering words of encouragement. I might have turned to them for help, but I felt awkward because Dave and I were supposed to be the lucky ones, and I dared not share how deeply I was hurting. How could I whine about the necessary inconveniences of success? Besides, there was nothing anyone could do to change the situation.

Six days after Tiffany's birth, I tucked her into her small wicker baby carrier and said good-bye to my friends. I wore my new dress, the one I had bought because my regular clothes were still far too small and my maternity clothes were too big.

Mary drove us to the airport in "Martha." As we drove past Waikiki Beach, it looked every bit the image of a picture postcard. Palm trees swayed in the breeze. White clouds drifted across the brilliant sky. I was going to miss Hawaii. I tried to drink in all the colors: the bronze skin tones of the people, the deep greens and earth tones shading the hillsides, the varied blues of sky and sea.

My feelings were so confused. I hated leaving our friends, who had been a great source of support over the past few years. But even though I struggled with the move, a sense of pride welled up inside me, too. I knew Dave and my mom would be so proud of me. Having a baby and moving on my own—that was quite an accomplishment.

Determined to take a more positive outlook, I gazed down at Tiffany fastened in her car seat. I had come through the most difficult part, and what lay ahead could be another grand adventure.

Mary walked slowly beside me, accommodating my careful steps as we moved up to the airline counter. With each step, I felt as though my stitches were ripping open, but I insisted on carrying Tiffany, enjoying the attention she received. *Yes,* I thought, *go ahead and look at my baby. She is beautiful, isn't she?*

One woman stared unabashedly at Tiffany and me. She looked to be in her fifties and wore tight blond-gray curls cropped close to her head. I smiled, fully expecting her compliments or good wishes.

"How old is that baby?" she asked brusquely.

"She's six days old." I'm sure I beamed with the pride I felt over Tiffany.

"You ought to be ashamed of yourself, taking a little baby like that to an airport. God only knows what kind of germs she could pick up. Why, I can't believe your mother let you do this."

I was dumbfounded. What did my mother have to do with this? I was a grown woman, capable of taking care of my baby.

Mary spoke up, putting her arm around my shoulder protectively. "She is taking this baby to see her father," she declared. With that said, she moved on briskly, taking me with her as fast as I could go, given my condition.

It felt so good having someone defending me, protecting me. Mary's protective love was the kind of love I needed so much at that time in my life. Coming to my defense was a simple gesture, but it meant the world to me at that moment. She was there for me when I needed her.

Now that I look back, I know the woman at the airport probably meant well. In her own way she was trying to offer protection too. Maybe if my mother had been there with me, she would have cautioned me to wait until Tiffany was a little older before taking her out. But my mother and my husband were far away across an ocean, and I was only doing what I thought I had to do, moving closer to those I loved, trusting that their love would provide a source of protective comfort for me and my baby.

When I arrived in San Diego, Dave was at the stadium, so Dave's parents met me at the airport. What a happy time! Not only were we rejoicing over Dave's move to the majors, but we were also celebrating the birth of their first grandchild.

While this was a happy time, I was still feeling the discomfort of recovering from giving birth just a week before. On top of that,

I had to move into the hotel the team provided—which was not exactly clean enough for a newborn—and find an apartment for our semi-permanent home. Oh, how I wished I could see my mom and dad!

My wishes were granted when my parents called and offered to fly Tiffany and me home to Ohio on July 4 for an entire week. None of this would have been possible had David stayed in triple-A ball in Hawaii.

When Tiffany was four weeks old, we flew home to be with my parents. As I deplaned, holding my baby, I immediately spotted my mother. Her dark eyes brimmed with joy, and we hugged, laughing and weeping. I had always been Mom's pride and joy. Now as I placed Tiffany in her arms, I knew I had finally returned some of that joy to her, just as I had always dreamed of doing.

My mother was of German ancestry, with a calm and sturdy demeanor. She was never gushy in her display of pleasant emotions. However, this was a moment she had waited for her whole life. She nestled Tiffany into her bosom as though it were a big pillow created just for this moment.

Turning to my dad, she bragged, "Honey, look at her. Oh, look at our precious little grandbaby. Can you believe Jan did this all on her own?"

All that week, Mom continued to brag about me to all her friends. "Can you believe Jan? Yeah, Dave goes into the majors, and she carries on all on her own. And she's doing so well with the baby." She was so pleased that I could take care of myself and that I'd given her this beautiful grandchild. Her high praise gave me strokes. Her confidence in me bolstered my confidence as well.

At that time in my life, my mother was my best friend. She was the one person who loved me for who I was. I could be ugly, and she'd still love me. She was the one I called about everything, sharing every crisis and every joy. We were happy just to spend time together.

The week passed far too quickly. When it came time to leave, I happened upon Mom standing in the hall. I wrapped my arms around her round frame and hugged her. "Mom, I love you," I told her.

Before we left, Mom insisted on holding Tiffany at every possible moment. But while we waited for my boarding call at the airport, she handed Tiffany to my dad. "Here, honey, will you take her? I'm too dizzy." I had never known my mother to get dizzy before, but I figured that all the excitement must have been getting to her.

Dave's parents followed us to the airport. Tiffany was their first grandchild, too, so they wanted to be there to see us off. It was a sunny day in Cleveland, and as I looked out of the window of the plane, my parents and Dave's parents stood at the gate, smiling and waving. As the plane taxied away, I waved back, feeling a sense of deep satisfaction and gratitude.

That was the best week I've ever spent with my mother—a precious gift of time from God. Little did I know, that would be the last time I would see my mother this side of heaven.

Four

I'm Fine, Really!

*T*hree weeks later, on July 31, 1982, Dave went to Cincinnati with the team. It was a big deal for us; because Riverfront stadium was only four hours from our hometown, family and friends could come to watch Dave pitch in the big leagues. This was a dream come true for Dave, and for his parents, who had taken him to Little League and watched him play ball in high school and college. Now they would sit in Riverfront stadium and watch their oldest son on the pitcher's mound. Dave's parents and mine would be in the stands, cheering him on—without me.

I wished I could be there with them and share their excitement. But I had just returned from Ohio, and we couldn't afford the airfare. Anyway, Tiffany was only seven weeks old, and I thought it best to refrain from another airplane trip. I settled for watching the game on TV.

The first six innings were great. We were ahead, but Dave had not yet played.

Then the announcer said, "Next up, Dave Dravecky, the young man from Youngstown."

I sat forward on the couch, brimming with excitement, trying to imagine what it must be like to be there in the stands at that moment with our parents. I bet they were having a ball. I could just see them sitting there, cheering with all their might. Even though I couldn't be there, I felt as though I was with them in spirit.

We won the game, with Dave pitching the last two innings, giving him his first major-league save. I could hardly wait for him to call so we could share his triumph, but this was the first game of a doubleheader. I would have to wait until the second game was over and give him time to clean up. So I decided to take a bath and bathe Tiffany while I waited.

About 10:30 a knock sounded at the door. It was Jackie Hawkins, my friend from Hawaii, whose husband had been called up to the majors a month after Dave. Glad to have someone to share my excitement, I chatted with her happily, never stopping to wonder why she had come over so late at night.

When the phone rang, I grabbed it on the first ring. "Dave," I cried. "You pitched a great game. I wish I could—"

He cut me off. "Janice, I have to tell you something."

"What?" His tone of voice stopped me cold.

"Janice, your mother died of a heart attack during the game."

I could not believe what I had just heard. "David, is this some kind of sick joke?" I asked.

"Jan, I would never joke about something like this."

Pain shot through me. Pain deeper and more horrible than any I had known. I don't know if seconds or minutes elapsed before I finally regained my composure.

I asked, "How did it happen?"

Dave explained, "They didn't tell me till the second game was over. It was a hot day, about ninety, and the humidity was probably just as high. It was miserable. The folks had walked quite a bit. I knew they were in the stands and tried to look their way while I was warming up. I noticed a commotion in the stands just before the seventh inning. I didn't pay much attention to it. Jan, it was your mom. The paramedics were trying to resuscitate her, but it was no use. She died instantly. My mom said she had seemed as happy as she had ever seen her. One minute she was laughing and talking. Then Mom looked over and she was . . . she was gone."

"Oh, David," I sobbed. "I wish you were here. I can't bear this alone."

"I know. I wish I could be there with you. That's why I had Jackie come over before I called. I didn't want you to be alone."

Now Jackie's silence made sense. She already had known about my mom and had come to comfort me. She had been there to share my joy at Tiffany's birth—now she was there to share my sorrow of my mom's death.

Jackie stayed with me that night and took me to the airport the next day. The flight home to Ohio was lonely and difficult. I didn't question God, but instead I felt a calm assurance that I had the promise of heaven. I'd only been a Christian for a year, but I sensed God's peace, what the Bible calls "the peace that passes all understanding." In spite of my devastating shock and pain, I had the assurance that I would see my mom again in heaven.

In the midst of this strange peace, I also felt the pressing need to take care of everyone and everything. I knew my dad and brother could not handle this without me, so I rallied myself to handle the funeral arrangements and console my family.

I felt so strange coming home without my mother there. Had it really been only three weeks since I felt her reassuring embrace while we stood there in that same hallway? I sat at the kitchen table, where we had shared a cup of tea. Those teacups were still in the cupboard, but my mom was gone.

I distinctly remembered one of our conversations during that wonderful week we spent together. I had said, "Mom, do you still love Dad?"

Her dark features softened as she became thoughtful. "Jan, I don't know if it's love in the same way you would describe your love for Dave. As your marriage grows and matures, a new kind of love develops. It's a kind of love that . . ."

I sipped at my tea while she searched for some way to explain the love to which she had devoted her life.

"It's like this," she continued. "It's like the two becoming one, so much so that if one partner was to lose the other you'd feel like you lost part of yourself. It's like an amputation, like losing part of your body."

"Is it romantic love?" I asked, feeling somewhat disappointed at her answer.

"Honey, I can't really tell you that I'm romantically in love with your father anymore. But if we were to be separated, it would be like losing my arm!"

As I recalled this conversation, I looked over at my poor father. I was saddened to see him in such pain. My father was a big, jolly man, but now he looked like an abandoned child. His eyes were downcast, and his big shoulders drooped. The life he had known was gone.

My brother was devastated, too. I stayed for three weeks in August and tried to take care of him and my father. I tried to teach my father how to live without his wife. I tried to help him put his life back together without the woman who had shared it for twenty-seven years.

At one point I broke down and cried, finally letting some of my sadness come to the surface. My father tried to console me in his own way.

"Janice, look at it this way. At least you still have your husband." He compared my pain over losing my mother to his grief at losing his wife, as if to lessen my grief by comparison.

"Besides," he said, "your mother wouldn't want you to fall apart. She never liked to see you cry. She'd want you to be happy."

I knew he was right about that. Mother always managed to steer me around any sadness. She wouldn't even let me watch *Lassie* because it sometimes made me cry.

After my conversation with my father, I stuffed the pain back down whenever it came up. People would ask, "Jan, how are you doing?"

I told them with all sincerity, "I'm fine, really. I'm fine."

I didn't want to cry. I didn't want to think about the pain, so I hid it. I did what a lot of people do: I got busy. I was torn between conflicting responsibilities. Dave wanted me to come home to San Diego. After all, we had an eleven-week-old daughter and had spent precious little time together as a family since she was born. But Dad also needed me. What should I do?

Finally, even though my mother was gone, I turned to her for wisdom. I asked myself, *What would Mom tell me to do?* She would have told me to go home to my own family—to be strong and continue pursuing the kind of life she always wanted for me. I recalled how proud she was of Tiffany and me, how pleased she was that Dave had finally achieved his goal. Even though I felt terribly guilty leaving my dad and my brother, I took my mom's advice.

Mom wanted me to walk in sunshine, not in shadows, so I decided to enjoy the journey upward. I devoted myself to God, my family, and Dave's career with fresh enthusiasm. The next five years in our baseball life were filled with success. Spiritually, we were growing. We received biblical teaching that laid a sure foundation for our understanding of God. (God knew we would need it more than we realized at the time.) We bought a house and established a permanent home in San Diego. Our lives were so easy. July 6, 1983, Dave was in the All-Star game. In October 1984, he was in the World Series. In 1985, Jonathan was born, and his birth was a bright contrast to Tiffany's. Dave was with me. I felt secure. I didn't insist on a natural birth this time, so I was able to manage the pain more easily. While in San Diego, we bought our dream home, faced financial ups and downs, and ended up selling our dream home to buy a house that was less of a financial burden. But overall, from 1982 to 1987, our lives flowed beautifully—until July 4, 1987.

On that day, Dave was traded from the San Diego Padres to the San Francisco Giants. I was devastated. I thought, *Lord, you've got it all wrong! I need to be closer to my father . . . Now you're moving me to San Francisco? San Francisco's not exactly where I want to live with my kids! If I move, I want to move east so I can be closer to my family.* My dad had remarried, but I still felt that he needed me.

But I was wrong—San Francisco would turn out to be one of the biggest blessings in my life. The people whom we met and the Christian fellowship we enjoyed there left long-lasting effects on us. In time we would come to see that the providence of God led us to San Francisco.

During the fall of 1987, Dave was at the top of his game, pitching in the playoffs and playing more consistently than ever before. He continued to amaze me, constantly surprising me with one achievement after another. I was so proud of him, I thought I might burst.

October 7, 1987, marked our ninth wedding anniversary. Dave was pitching in the National League Championship series against the St. Louis Cardinals. I could think of no greater way to celebrate our life together than to see him out there on the mound, whizzing balls past the plate in such an important game. He pitched a two-hitter to win the game 5–0.

When we found each other in the corridor of the stadium after the game, he practically picked me up. He took me in his arms and hugged me for all he was worth, and then he kissed me. At that moment, we had it all. We had a wonderful marriage. Dave had tremendous opportunities to share his faith because of his success. And we had two beautiful children, a nice home, and love to fill it. We were both overjoyed.

Laughing, I asked Dave, "How do you plan to top this?"

We had been shooting for the stars ever since we met, and even after nine years of marriage, we still had those stars in our eyes. We felt so blessed that we had been given the privilege of seeing those astronomical dreams come true. At this high point of our lives, we saw visions of grandeur. Dave and I both believed that 1988 was going to be our year. We believed he could win twenty games that year, the ultimate for any major league pitcher.

We had no way of knowing how different those visions would appear from the valley of the shadow of death. We would learn soon enough.

Five

At the Crossroads

*A*t the end of 1987, I had a plan for my life and for where I wanted God to take us. God had a plan too. His plan and mine were not the same. Of course, I had no way of knowing that at the time. I didn't realize that God was about to lead me to a crossroads where I would have to make a choice. Would I choose to continue on my own journey or follow him on a journey not my own?

Dave and I had hopes for twenty wins in 1988, but a shoulder injury put Dave on the disabled list. Dave had surgery to repair a torn ligament in his shoulder and was in continual pain.

We consoled ourselves with one of our favorite Bible verses: "And we know that in all things God works for the good of those who love him, who have been called according to his purpose. For those God foreknew he also predestined to be conformed to the likeness of his Son, that he might be the firstborn among many brothers" (Romans 8:28–29). We took that promise to mean that whatever happened, God would work the situation out to our advantage. But God's priorities were not ours. Our priority was to continue to enjoy a happy, comfortable life. His priority was to conform us to the image and likeness of his Son, Jesus.

Before God could conform me to his image, he had to tear down the false images of him I had already set up in my mind. The first commandment says, "You shall have no other gods before me." I never thought much about that commandment because I didn't realize I was breaking it. But, growing up, I fashioned an image of God out of bits and pieces of the Bible.

I wasn't like ancient peoples who fashioned a statue of some god created in their own imagination, then prayed for it to grant their wishes. But idolatry doesn't have to involve sculpting a statue; it can be sculpting an image of a god as one wants God to be, a god who lives to obey our directions. And that's what I did. This God I created conveniently fit into my plans and never interfered with my desires, even when those desires violated the moral code in the Bible.

Time and again God has taken me through experiences that caused my false images of him to crumble, so I could see him as he really is. Every time I see him more clearly, I am changed to become more like him. The image I hold of God has changed dramatically over the past fifteen years, and I have changed with it.

God had quite a job to do to change me to become more like his Son. Jesus was a man of sorrows and acquainted with grief, but part of my life plan was to stay as far away as possible from suffering and sadness. This is where his plans and mine have been at cross-purposes time after time.

The first time God started taking me on his journey came even before I was a Christian. It was in 1979 when Dave and I were first married. Dave was playing Double-A ball for the Pittsburgh Pirates. I'll never forget the day Dave came home and said, "They're sending me to winter ball." I saw this as a big step up for Dave because it meant that management thought he showed promise. I thought, *I can't believe it. The Lord has given me my wish.*

I had heard stories from other baseball wives whose husbands played ball in Puerto Rico and Venezuela. When Dave said they were sending us to Colombia, I envisioned a Caribbean paradise. I imagined sunning myself on a beautiful beach all winter. Now I can't believe I was so naive.

At that time I imagined God as this big granddaddy in the sky who blessed people when they were good and punished them when they were bad. I believed that life was fair, and since I'd never gone outside the United States, I believed that people all over the world lived as we did. At twenty-three, I was about as ignorant as a person can get. Now I was moving to a third-world country, thinking I was in for the time of my life.

I remember flying into Colombia and looking down at the coca fields. I didn't know what they were at the time, but I now know that coca is used to make cocaine. I remember seeing grass shacks in the fields. I thought, *Oh, how cute! Look at all those little grass shacks. That must be where they house their animals.* I was soon to learn *people* lived in those shacks.

I was shocked by the poverty. Baranquilla is an industrial city of about two million people. About ninety-five percent of them are poor beyond any comprehension that we have of poor in the United States. And five percent are extremely rich. The majority of the rich are the drug barons who live on the outside of town on large gated estates. The gates are made of pure green jade. The stark contrast between rich and poor was a devastating sight and a real eye opener for this spoiled American.

There was such a disregard for life. I saw a man on a motorcycle hit by a car and killed. They just threw his body in the back of a truck like a piece of meat. Men stood on corners with machine guns. People couldn't go to the bank without openly carrying a gun because it was so unsafe to walk the streets.

Medical care is very archaic compared to that available in the United States. A Colombian native on our team watched his child die of dysentery. In the United States the child would have been given medication and been fine. His child dehydrated and died because of lack of provisions.

I had taken so much for granted in life, but in Colombia the comforts of home are rare commodities. To have enough electricity to light the ballpark, city officials shut off the current to half of the city. The water was turned off for long periods without warning or explanation. The sewers would flood and run outside our apartment building, the smell rising up into our apartment. Our apartment had no hot water. We couldn't call home because only about thirty-nine lines went outside the entire country. So we felt totally cut off from our family and from the United States. On top of that, I contracted parasites and was terribly sick the entire time we were there.

Seeing the unfairness and thinking about the suffering I witnessed caused my image of God to crumble into dust and blow away. When it did, I had nothing left to believe in. Obviously no big granddaddy existed in the sky who blessed those who did good and punished those who were bad. If there was, then why were so many good people in Colombia suffering? Why were they dying for no good reason? Why were the wicked people, the drug barons, allowed to live like kings? I thought life was supposed to be fair, but this certainly was not fair!

I grew up experiencing a close relationship with God, always feeling the presence of God in my life. By the time I returned to the United States, however, I faced serious doubts for the first time. I felt as though I'd been lied to my whole life. The God that I grew up knowing was a God of love. How could a God of love allow what I had seen in Colombia? And if there was no God, then who was in charge?

I had never felt so alone as I did at that time. Nothing made sense anymore. I could not bear the thought that this life meant nothing, but my image of God was destroyed and I had nothing with which to replace it. So I got busy and distracted myself with activity. I didn't want to think. I didn't want to ask questions that had no comfortable answers. I didn't want to do anything that would remind me of God.

For the first time in my life I quit going to church. At the same time during the 1980 season, Dave started going to baseball chapel every Sunday. He was hearing about a personal relationship with Jesus Christ while I was moving away from God. Yet neither of us knew what the other was doing, because we didn't share our spiritual lives.

During the winter of 1980–81, Dave and I moved to Sarasota, Florida. I went to work for an accounting firm, working long hours and trying to save money for a down payment on a house while trying to keep myself busy so I would not have to think. Dave had promised he would never play winter ball again, but when he was asked again, management insisted that he go. So off he went—this time without me.

Dave was lonely and scared in Colombia, but God was drawing Dave to him. Dave's roommates were Christians and held Bible studies. He watched and listened, and seeds of faith were planted.

That spring of 1981 when Dave was traded to the San Diego Padres and sent to Amarillo, Texas, I stayed behind in Florida to work and save money. Dave's roommate, Byron Ballard, was a Christian. Byron challenged Dave to read the Bible. Because of his Catholic upbringing, Dave did honor God's Word and had no doubt the Bible was the true Word of God; the only problem was that he'd never read it before. As he read, he was amazed at what it had to say, how we're all sinners who have fallen short of the glory of God. He was shocked to learn that the wages of sin is death (even for nice people). Dave was relieved to find that he could receive forgiveness through believing in Jesus Christ and be assured of eternal life.

As he learned all this, Dave grew very excited. He does not have a calm personality, and when he becomes passionate about something, he wants to share it. And if Jesus was good enough for Dave, Dave thought Jesus was good enough for everyone!

So Dave called me and told me everything he was learning—right when any thought of God caused me pain. I had kept as busy as I could, filling my life so I wouldn't have to think about God. And Dave was calling me every night, telling me something else that he had learned about God. I did not want to hear it!

Finally I said to him, "What have you done, David? What are you involved in? Please don't do anything until I get there."

When I got to Amarillo, Dave was extremely forceful, and all I remember saying to him was, "Bug off! You're not going to force this down my throat. If it's the truth, I'll learn to accept it, but if it's not, I'm not going to believe because you told me to."

Dave backed off—a miracle in itself. And slowly, tentatively, I began to explore the claims of the Bible for myself.

I started going to Bible study and by the end of summer, God answered my first question: Why is there suffering? I understood for the first time about the fall of humanity. I learned that sin brought a curse on the world, a curse that affects us all. I learned that God sends the sunshine and rain on good and bad alike. The state of the world started to make sense. I was shown where the Bible says that life is not fair; the strongest don't always win the battle, nor do the swiftest always win the race. I came to understand that ultimately, life will be fair after God does his accounting, when we arrive in our heavenly home.

During that time, I accepted Christ into my life. I say, "I accepted Christ into my life," rather than "I gave my life to Christ," because I didn't really give my life to Christ. I willingly accepted Jesus because I could see the truth of his claims and the changes he had made in Dave's life. Accepting Christ also relieved the terrible void left when my previous image of God was blown away. However, I still retained control of my life.

God began to shatter that control when Dave discovered cancer in his pitching arm.

In the fall of 1987, after Dave had pitched the two best games of his career in the playoffs, he noticed a small lump on his arm. I thought nothing of it. The doctors told us it was probably scar tissue. That seemed to make sense because, though we could not recall a specific incident, a pitcher is prone to injure his pitching arm. In January of 1988, Dave had an MRI (magnetic resonant imaging), and the results were inconclusive. So we assumed that everything was fine. We didn't think God would let anything terrible happen in our lives.

That small lump in Dave's pitching arm seemed irrelevant; it had nothing to do with my plans. Because of Dave's success on the mound, we had opportunities to share our faith with others through the media, and I thought God wanted me to share my faith with women as opportunities arose. It seemed God had given me a gift for speaking, and I thought that could make me useful in God's hands. (Now, I realize how far I was from understanding what makes one truly useful in the hands of God.) God had done so much for us; I wanted to do something for him in return. God had lifted us up, and I thought he would keep us on top. Then we would give glory to God, unashamedly before the watching world. That's what we thought God would do, and that fit nicely in my plans.

In the summer of 1988, we were living in San Francisco in a rented home. We still owned our home in San Diego, where we lived during the off-season, and we also were building a home in Ohio. Dave had been on the disabled list since June 11, when he had arthroscopic surgery for a torn tendon in his shoulder. He was disappointed that he had not performed as he had hoped for the Giants, and I was longing for home. So we decided to move our home base back to Ohio, even though we would still live near the team during baseball season.

Spiritually, we felt as though we were at a standstill at this time in our lives. We both sensed that something was still coming between God and us. Jesus said to his disciples, "If anyone would

come after me, he must deny himself and take up his cross and follow me." We knew we weren't sold out to that extent. We didn't
have the slightest desire to be crucified, but we wanted to follow
Jesus. So we prayed together, "Dear God, we want to surrender
totally to you. Lord, we know we're not to the point where we
would be willing to take up a cross and follow you. But we want
you to bring us to that point. Please change our hearts to make us
willing to deny ourselves and follow you wherever you lead us."

I had no idea the impact that prayer would have.

The season was winding down, and Dave wasn't playing
because of the problems with his shoulder. I decided to take the
kids back home to Ohio, where we were living with Dave's parents
while our house was being built. I wanted to get the kids settled
before school started in September, and Dave would follow shortly.
Before he left to come home, the Giants' doctor, Dr. Gordon
Campbell, suggested that Dave undergo another set of MRI tests
on the lump in his arm. It had been more than six months since it
had been last examined, and the lump had grown to the size of a
golf ball. He had the tests done on September 9, then flew home
the next day.

A few days later, Dr. Campbell called. There was a soft tissue
mass on the end of Dave's deltoid muscle. He had some specialists
look at the test results and suggested that Dave see a doctor in our
area. He recommended Dr. Bergfeld, the team doctor for the
Cleveland Indians, and offered to make the appointment for him.

The next day, September 19, 1988, we went to the Cleveland
Clinic. I didn't have any sense of apprehension. It just seemed like
another doctor's appointment. I knew they were questioning the
nature of the lump, but I wasn't anxious. We had been through this
before in January. I was very concerned then, but that turned out
to be nothing. So this time felt like a routine checkup.

The examining room was tiny. Dave sat on the examining table
while I sat on a chair. Several doctors and medical personnel

paraded in and out, asking a series of questions, filling out medical histories and various forms. One group had Dave take his shirt off. They examined his left arm, had him rotate it, then felt the muscle and the lump.

We began to wonder how many preliminary formalities and procedures we'd have to go through before we actually got to meet Dr. Bergfeld. I was somewhat nervous, not because of the medical concerns, but because of Dr. Bergfeld's reputation. He was the orthopedic surgeon for the Cleveland Browns and the Cleveland Indians. Besides, if the number of medical personnel preceding his arrival was an indication of the doctor's importance, then we were about to meet a very important man.

We heard a door open in the room next to us. Several voices carried on conversation in low tones, just loud enough to indicate that Dr. Bergfeld had arrived but not loud enough for us to hear what was being discussed. Dave and I looked at each other. We could hear papers shuffling and the footsteps of what seemed to be several people. Then we heard them slap the film from Dave's MRI onto the light board. Automatically we fell silent, trying to overhear what they were saying.

Then one voice came through low and clear. "Look at the tumor."

Tumor? Did he say . . . *tumor?* I looked at Dave to see if he had heard. His expression told me that he had. In that instant, shock stood guard over my heart and mind to keep the terrifying fear away for a few moments more.

"David, we better pray."

"Yeah," he said. "We better pray right now."

He lost no time getting off the examining table and into the chair beside me. We held hands as he prayed. "Dear God, we don't know what's happening. We don't know what this means. But please help us get through it, no matter what is involved. Help us face whatever comes. Amen."

Facing "whatever comes" had never been my strong suit, especially if "whatever comes" might be painful. I was far better at *not*
facing whatever comes. In that respect, I was like Scarlett O'Hara.
Whenever tragedy threatened, I preferred to think about it . . .
tomorrow.

However, a surprising thing happened at that moment as I sat
in that little exam room. I didn't look toward tomorrow with unrealistic optimism. Instead, for a fleeting instant I recalled the prayer
Dave and I had prayed the month before. We wanted to surrender
totally to God. Could we surrender to him while facing the threat
of cancer? We asked God to change our hearts to make us willing
to deny ourselves and follow him wherever he might lead. Could
this be "wherever he might lead"? Could this be our cross to bear?
If so, I did not feel ready.

Ready or not, I had to face whatever was to come. Dr. Bergfeld
strode into the room and greeted us with a warm handshake.

Dr. Bergfeld was a jovial man who put me at ease immediately.
I thought it odd that such a happy man should bring such unsettling news. He explained that we were not dealing with scar tissue,
but a tumor. He seemed to understand our unspoken fears. He
calmly explained to Dave that he didn't know if the tumor was
malignant because it had been present for over a year, and its rate
of growth was much slower than might be expected if it was malignant. He referred us to an oncologist, Dr. Muschler, on the fifth
floor who agreed that Dave should have a biopsy.

Two days later, Dave had the biopsy. Two days after that we
received word that Dave's tumor was a desmoid tumor. My cousin,
Mark Roh, who is a cancer surgeon, explained to me that Dave had
cancer, but it was a tumor that was unlikely to spread through the
body. It would grow and spread locally, but it wasn't life-threaten-
ing if treated with aggressive surgery. The doctors needed to
remove every last cell of the tumor, and that put Dave's pitching
arm at risk.

Dave's mom, Donna, went with Dave and me when we returned to the Cleveland Clinic to discuss the biopsy results with Dr. Muschler. He confirmed what Mark had already told me. In addition, he told us that a desmoid tumor was the most likely to come back after being surgically removed. He explained that one single cancer cell left behind could grow into another tumor, and they would have to cut a wide margin of muscle around the tumor to make sure they removed every last cancer cell. Dr. Muschler prepared us for the likelihood that they might have to remove half of Dave's deltoid muscle—the large muscle in his upper pitching arm.

The problem was the humerus bone on which the tumor rested. Dr. Muschler didn't believe the tumor had actually invaded the bone, but the most conservative approach would be to cut away half or all of the bone beneath the tumor and reconstruct it with bone from the bone bank at the Cleveland Clinic.

Muschler preferred another option. He could cut right down to the very edge of the bone, and then freeze the portion of the tumor near the bone, using liquid nitrogen. That would kill all living cells, even living bone cells, but it would make surgery considerably less destructive and recovery much faster. With this freezing technique, called cyrosurgery, the bone would be brittle and for some time liable to break. But it would eventually recover its full strength.

After we questioned Dr. Muschler fully, considering every medical angle, Dave asked, "What about my career?"

Dr. Muschler quietly replied, "Well, Dave, if you have this operation, I think your chances of returning to professional baseball are zero."

We decided to proceed with the surgery. There seemed no other reasonable option.

On October 7, 1988, our tenth wedding anniversary, Dave, his mother, and I arrived at the hospital at the time appointed for the surgery. He went in at 6:00 A.M. for an operation that was supposed to take approximately four hours.

The hospital waiting room was filled with anxious people whose loved ones were undergoing surgery. Overhead, the hospital TV offered a distraction, but it offered no relief for us. The National League playoffs were on the screen, and Dave wasn't on the mound. He was in a room down the hall, where a surgeon was carving away the muscles in his pitching arm. And if the doctor's prognosis was accurate, we would never see him on the mound again.

Everyone deals with fear and grief differently. I found relief by talking. It seemed that by discussing every aspect of what Dave was going through, I gained some control over the concepts, if not the actual problems. However, Donna didn't want to think or talk about the details of what was happening to her son. She found any discussion of the matter too painful to bear. She wanted to be there for Dave, but she wanted to remain quiet while doing so.

Dave's dad, Frank, couldn't bear to wait in the hospital, so Donna and I were left to each other's care. Our differing ways of coping made it difficult for us to comfort each other. She tried to withdraw. I tried to sort out all the details verbally, as though I could figure out some way to make them balance. We both waited.

After four hours, I approached the nurse's station several times to ask if Dave was out of surgery yet. Each time I asked, hour after hour, they had nothing to report. At 6:00 P.M. the doctor came out. He looked exhausted as he approached us. "We're going to have to take Dave back in for emergency surgery on his leg," he explained.

The surgery had taken far longer than they had expected. It had gone well, but Dave was lying on his right side for the entire time, which had cut off circulation to his leg. When they turned him over after the surgery, the rush of blood back into his leg created tremendous pressure, and they had to do another surgery, slicing open the muscle to relieve the pressure on his leg. Dave was in terrible pain, not only in his arm but also in his leg.

Donna and I were left to ourselves in the waiting room while Dave was taken back into surgery. I looked around; the room was empty now except for the two of us, sitting silently side by side and watching the New York Mets play the Los Angeles Dodgers in the race for the National League pennant. I kept my thoughts to myself. *How could there be so much change in one year? Was it really only one year ago today that Dave was pitching a winning game in the playoffs?* I dared not express these thoughts, even if Donna had been in the mood to talk. The picture was too ironic, too confusing, far too painful.

Finally, at 8:20, Dr. Muschler came through the doors. We rushed to him, anxious for a good report.

"The surgery went well," he said.

"Can we see him?" we asked.

"Yes, you can see him for a few minutes in the recovery room, but then I suggest you go home and get some sleep."

I didn't want to upset Donna, but I had to know the details of what had happened to Dave's arm. I was always the one who kept track of the details. Even when he was playing, I kept track of all the statistics. Back then I was calculating his earned-run average; now I was calculating the chances Dave would ever pitch again.

"Dr. Muschler, I need to know," I said. "Tell me exactly what you did and what it means."

He patiently explained, "We did have to remove fifty percent of the deltoid muscle, as I expected. We went layer by layer, but we found it necessary to—"

I interrupted, "What about the bone?"

"We froze the bone, as I explained we would. The bone cells will die, but in time new cells will replace those and the bone will eventually regenerate."

"What about Dave's career?"

His look was one of resignation and exhaustion as he shook his head.

I interpreted for him. "So what you're saying is that Dave will never pitch again." I knew the answer might be hard for Donna to hear, but I had to know. I had to hear it straight and clear, in some form I could calculate. "What are his chances of pitching again professionally?"

Dr. Muschler looked into my eyes. I distinctly recall his young, weary face as he said, "No, Jan, he probably won't be able to pitch again. My dream of a successful recovery would be for Dave to play catch with Jonathan one day. But outside of a miracle, Dave will never pitch again professionally."

There are moments in my life when memories are so distinct they are like photographs of thoughts and feelings; all the details are clearly in mind. This conversation with Dr. Muschler on my tenth wedding anniversary was one of those "snapshot" moments. Another one was from our ninth anniversary, when Dave held me in his arms in the corridor of the stadium and I asked him, "Now how are you going to top this?" Now these two snapshots, taken exactly one year apart, were pinned up side by side in the gallery of my heart.

I knew this was no mere coincidence, but I was too emotionally spent to figure anything out just then. Yet I did sense a strange assurance that this was part of the journey. God was calling me to follow his plans, not my own. Cancer was definitely not in my plan. But for some reason, God had allowed it to invade our lives.

I had made a decision to follow Jesus through whatever was to come, and I would continue to follow him. Somehow, I knew that God would cause all things to work together for good—even when one of those things was cancer.

Six

∞

Something Bigger Than Baseball

The doctors told us that Dave would need therapy to recover the use of his left arm at even the most basic level. Something as simple as raising his arm above his head or taking his wallet out of his back pocket would be a major accomplishment. Dave would have to learn to use other muscles to do what his deltoid muscle used to do. The medical staff at the Cleveland Clinic prepared us for a long, slow, and demanding recovery.

Since I'm a planner, I came up with a plan. Tiffany was six, and Jonathan was three, and I was committed to staying home to raise them. So I thought, *Dave needs to get a real job*, and I started planning his life for him.

When an athletic director from a college in the Midwest called to discuss a coaching position, I was eager for Dave to call him back. I kept after him to return the call, but he kept putting it off. Dave was focused on dealing with the pain and recovering from his surgery. But somewhere deep down inside, something else kept him from making that call. He was holding on to the hope that something miraculous would happen. He had always viewed himself as an underdog, a guy who overcomes all the obstacles, defying the odds. Neither could Dave's parents accept that his career was over. I seemed to be the only one thinking realistically about our future.

The third time Dave refused to call about the coaching job, I tried to help him face reality.

"David," I said, "you have to start thinking about what you are going to do for a career. You're going to have to get some kind of job."

He frowned. "Janice, we don't have to think about that right now. Let's just see how things go."

I knew this wasn't going to be an easy transition for him. That's why I was trying to help him with it. "Dave, let's be serious. You need to think about coaching or something else. You have to start thinking about another career."

That made him angry. "Look, don't count me out just yet!"

That hurt! I believed in my husband. I've always worked hard to give him whatever kind of support he needed. But after what Dr. Muschler had said, I focused my faith in him in another direction. I would have been the first to encourage him if that were a reasonable thing to do. And it wasn't that I didn't believe in miracles. I knew God could do miracles, but for whatever reason, God had allowed this to happen. Now we just had to make the best of it.

Dave's response showed me that he was not ready to face life without baseball. I hoped and prayed that he would come around and be able to make a positive adjustment. But he wasn't ready to discuss it further, so I let it go.

On October 20, 1988, thirteen days after his surgery, Dave came into the room and said, "Look at this." Then he raised his left arm over his head. He wasn't supposed to be able to do that. His look said, "See, I told you!"

I gasped. "Dave, you're not supposed to be able to do that!"

"I know, but I just did," he said, grinning triumphantly.

I didn't know what to think or feel. I was amazed to see Dave recovering so quickly.

Less than six weeks after the surgery, I was at the sink, washing dishes, when Dave sauntered into the kitchen with a broad grin on his face. I turned around to see what he was up to.

"Watch this," he said. Then he slowly took his left hand, reached around to his back pocket, removed his wallet, and held it up for me to see.

I squealed, "Dave, Dave, I can't believe it!" Then the tears came, tears of astonishment and joy. That simple movement was something the doctors had said he wouldn't be able to do without intense therapy.

"That's not all." His triumphant grin never faded. "Watch this." And there in my kitchen I witnessed a small miracle. Ever so slowly, Dave took his left arm through his pitching motion. I knew that God was doing something. I stood corrected. Once again, Dave Dravecky had proven to me that I should never count him out. And nothing could have made me happier.

I still knew we had to take it one day at a time, but my focus changed the moment Dave gave that dramatic demonstration. He later joked that showing me he could go through his pitching motion was a big mistake. From that moment on, I didn't let up. If Dave was going to try to make a comeback, I was determined to do everything in my power to encourage him. His rehabilitation consisted of grueling workouts with free weights and strenuous physical therapy. I made sure that he went every day. At times he didn't want to go, but I considered it my wifely duty to make sure he went even if I had to kick him out the door—and some days, I did!

I wanted Dave to succeed, but I wanted security, too. Part of me hoped he would make a comeback; another part of me wanted him to have another secure career we could count on. I wanted to flip to the end of his story and read the last page, but I couldn't. I was going to have to walk through his recovery, one day at a time, and that went against my whole being. While I encouraged Dave in his rehabilitation, I still kept after him to consider another career beyond baseball. But he just kept getting better and better and better.

By March 1989, he was throwing. I couldn't believe it. In April we locked up our house in Ohio, rented a townhouse in San Francisco, and rejoined the San Francisco Giants. By June, Dave was throwing pitches across the plate; by July, he was in competition. They sent him back to the minor leagues to work his way back up. I'd never seen a happier guy. He was acting like a kid, just thrilled to be out on the field again playing the game he loved. We were both so grateful that he had the chance to play again. We never doubted that it was a gift from God.

The degree of media attention and support from the fans surprised us. In Stockton, California, at Dave's first minor league game, 4,500 people crammed into bleachers made to seat a lot less. Reporters were everywhere. They were all so supportive, so encouraged by the miracles we were all watching unfold before our eyes. Dave's prayer at the time was "Thank you, God, that I have the chance to play again. If I never play another game after this one, I'm still grateful. This is enough, but if you want me to come back, open the door."

For the next step on Dave's road to a major-league comeback, the Giants sent him to Phoenix to play with the triple-A team there. The media attention continued as Dave pitched three winning games in the minor leagues. It seemed obvious that he was ready, so management promoted him back up to the majors. It had been ten months and three days since his surgery.

While he was recovering, friends introduced Dave to Alex Vlahos, a young boy with leukemia at Stanford Children's hospital. Dave visited Alex at the hospital, where they bonded instantly. Alex was a baseball fan, and Dave enjoyed tossing a few pitches his way.

Alex was thrilled to get a hit off a real major-league pitcher. It was such a small thing for Dave to do, and yet it meant so much to Alex and his family.

A San Francisco radio station caught wind of the comeback before it happened. They also heard about how Dave had been visiting Alex. So the DJs at KNBR asked listeners to call in pledges to help offset medical expenses for Alex. They raised pledges amounting to a thousand dollars for every pitch Dave would throw that day. I thought that was a wonderful idea, but I also thought, *Oh, great. Let's add pressure to an already pressured game.*

Nobody was more surprised than I when Dave was able to throw again on August 10, 1989. It amazed us both. But what amazed us even more was the response from the fans. When Dave came out of the tunnel and onto the field, some 37,000 fans packing the stadium went wild. Before the game even started, they were cheering like someone had hit a home run—and that included the fans of the opposing team. Everybody seemed overwhelmed with the wonder of what we were seeing. Dave had beat the odds, and everyone loved it.

The media attention was overwhelming, too. Reporters lined the fence. Every major network and every small station seemed to have someone covering that game. The eyes of the world were on Dave Dravecky, and we knew it was only by the grace of God.

Inning after inning, Dave made one great pitch after another. In all, he threw 115 pitches that day. The crowd couldn't seem to stay in their seats. I counted at least nine standing ovations, each one more generous than the last. When the light board flashed the sign in giant letters WELCOME BACK, DAVE, I could barely contain my joy. The tears streamed down my face as I stood and clapped along with everyone else.

Roger Craig, the Giants' manager, said that in all his decades playing and managing, he had never seen so much intense emotion at a game. He was right. The sense of shared celebration we all felt at the triumph of one man over adversity was powerfully inspirational. As I stood there clapping and cheering, I remembered one of those snapshots, forever mounted in my heart and mind: the one where Dr. Muschler told me that, outside of a miracle, Dave would never pitch again. And here he was, standing on the mound, having thrown over one hundred great pitches. I was in shock. I think I doubted it until it actually happened. Dave and I knew this was a miracle. From the way everybody else was cheering, I think they knew it, too.

Dave pitched seven great innings and only gave up one hit. We won the game, too. He earned $115,000 for Alex and helped draw attention to the need for bone marrow donors. Over 18,000 people signed up as possible donors because of the media attention associated with Dave's comeback. We were awed at how wonderfully God had caused all things to work together for good.

That night before we went to bed, we kneeled on opposite sides of the bed and started to pray. Then Dave halted. I raised my head to see him looking at me, wearing this expression of wonder and astonishment in his eyes, his whole face smiling.

"Jan, can you believe it? Do you realize what took place today?"

"I know; I can't believe it, David! But it happened!"

We finished praying, but we just kept shaking our heads at the wonder of it all. We never in our wildest dreams imagined anything so grand. It was beyond us.

The media seemed to be in a frenzy. Publishers were calling, wanting us to write a book. Producers were calling, wanting to do a movie. Everyone wanted an interview. And in those interviews, Dave was talking about what the Lord had done. Usually, reporters try to steer away from faith issues, especially in sports interviews. Everyone had to admit, though, that without God, Dave Dravecky could never have made this comeback. It was such a tremendous opportunity to share Christ with people. Dave was so excited about how God would use this miracle in his life and how his testimony of what God had done was going to be printed in the paper.

Dave's next scheduled game was in Montreal on August 15, against the Expos. I stayed in California, three thousand miles away. The game wasn't being televised, so Dave's parents and I got together to listen to the game on the radio. It was hot, and the kids were getting restless, so we took the radio out to the pool. That way, the kids could swim while we listened to the game.

I get very intense when I'm listening to Dave's games. So it worked out well to have the kids in the pool while we listened in our lounge chairs. The game was going well. We were ahead, and Dave was on the mound in the sixth inning.

The announcer's voice boomed, "At the plate, Tim Raines. And here's the pitch . . . and Dave Dravecky falls over . . ." His voice rose anxiously. "Dravecky stumbled on the mound . . . threw a wild pitch . . . Hank, he's holding his arm. He's down."

At that first instant, I was shocked but figured he'd just stumbled and was trying to protect his arm.

The announcer's voice went on, "The players are coming out onto the field. I can't see Dravecky. He's surrounded by players from the Giants and . . . the players from the Expos are on the field too . . ."

Then I knew it was serious. The other team never came out onto the field unless it was serious. I jumped up, as though I could do something. Dave's parents and I were frantic to find out what had happened. Immediately we started making phone calls.

I should have been a complete basket case, but something strange happened. When we got word that Dave had broken his arm, I was overwhelmed—not with fear or anger or sadness—but with a feeling of excitement. I didn't feel cheated even though he had worked for the past year to get back on that mound. I was in awe . . . I was in awe that he hadn't broken his arm before this. He started throwing in April. Why didn't his arm break then? Why was he allowed to pitch three minor league games and win each one, then pitch in the majors and have a fantastic game? It wasn't just that he pitched; he pitched great! But then, while all the world's eyes were on him, admiring him, praising him for his accomplishments, he falls from the mound and breaks his arm.

I can't explain how I knew, but I knew God was in it.

Later, when Dave was able to call, he told me his side of things. When Dave released the ball, it felt like an ax had slashed his arm in two. As he fell to the ground, all he could think about was something Bob Knepper had said to him a few hours before the game.

Bob is a close friend who was signed to the Giants two weeks before. Dave had been talking with Bob about the excitement over God's using this miracle in his life and how it was going to be printed in the paper. Bob looked at him and said, "You know, Dave, I hate to burst your bubble, but what about the miracle of salvation that took place in your life seven years ago? That's what you have to share. God has given you a platform through baseball, but it's to share about salvation, not just your comeback."

When Dave told me this on the phone, he was in a lot of pain, but he was strangely excited, too. He said to me, "Jan, when I fell from the mound, even though the pain was almost too much to bear, Bob's words came back to me. I was overcome with a sense of God's presence, a strong assurance that God was doing something. . . ." Then he paused as if to take it all in. "I knew God was doing something far bigger than baseball. All I could feel was awe, as though I had a new, even more exciting goal."

Dave and I refer to that shared moment of realization—that God was doing something special—as our vision. Three thousand miles apart, we had been given a supernatural sense of God's providential care at a moment of tragedy. That vision was a powerful indication to both of us that God had taken our prayers to surrender our lives to him far more seriously than we realized he would. Already we had a sense of expectancy, wondering what great things God would do next.

In the Old Testament, whenever God did something of significance for the Israelites, something he didn't want them to forget, he had them build a monument so that they would remember. Dave's comeback and his fall from the mound became monuments in our lives.

This vision was given to us on August 16, 1989. What was to come afterward was unknown. At this point all we knew was that we were to commemorate God's tremendous miracle in our lives, and he sealed it by giving us this sense of shared vision.

We didn't even have *our* plans anymore. What happened from here on out was up to God. The team doctor, Dr. Campbell, saw no reason that Dave could not recover and come back to pitch again, but we ourselves didn't know what would happen next. Just a year ago, we had surrendered ourselves completely to God and asked him to lead us in his will. What God took us through in that year was beyond anything we could have imagined, but because of our shared vision we trusted that God's will would prevail. But neither of us was sure now what God's will might be—or where he would lead us next.

Seven

Wonder Woman Put to the Test

*O*ur phone constantly rang off the hook after Dave broke his arm on August 15, 1989. We experienced a media blitz, with newspaper and TV reporters calling for interviews. All our friends called, too, wanting to see how we were, wish us well, or offer advice.

We felt an exciting rush of emotion. You know how one week something takes place, and the next week they've got a movie out about it? Well, publishers and producers from all across the country offered us an unbelievable amount of money to do this or that. *Wow!* Dave was on the cover of *USA TODAY* several times. He was on *The Today Show* and *Good Morning, America. People* magazine and many others wanted to do a story.

We were in a quandary. We had so many offers, all requiring a decision and a response. We had a difficult time because most of the people were so nice and the things asked of us were good! We simply had too many offers. Some people even called to tell us that God had told them what we were supposed to do. We didn't want to say no to anyone, but we had to make choices.

We felt caught in a trap: Number one, it made us feel better to say yes, and number two we didn't feel like we had the right to say no, that we had to say yes to be true, self-sacrificing Christians. Dave and I wanted to please everyone. We thought, *Here are all of these needs. We can't possibly meet them all. So, what are we going to do?* We weren't even sure *how* to make our decisions.

Our garage in San Francisco was filled with mail up to my knees. We received so many wonderful letters: stories about cancer, about someone breaking his arm, cards of encouragement. We were so touched by the response of the American public. Unbelievable gifts kept coming, not just from people who wanted us to do things but from people who just have big hearts.

I'm used to giving, not receiving, and my gut-level response was "Oh, someone sent me this gift; I need to send something back!" This inner pressure to reciprocate made me feel that more was being asked of me than I could give. I was no longer trying to please only my family and friends; suddenly, I felt that I had to please the American public. I had always been confident that I could handle my life, and at a certain level I could. But my attempt to reciprocate such overwhelming kindness was utterly ridiculous. It was almost like a joke, as though the Lord exaggerated the situation to show me how ridiculous it was to try to do it all. But I wasn't getting the point, and my life was spinning out of control.

Beyond the obvious requests, I realized the media was hungry for a hero. Hey, I'd heard the song. I was supposed to be the wind beneath Dave's wings. So I felt I should help Dave maintain the image people expected from him.

You know what they say, "Behind every good man there's a good woman!" That's how it was with us. Other than Dave's actually playing baseball, I was used to running his life; I ran our home, family, everything. To my way of thinking, Dave didn't have time to do all that. This attitude goes back to my upbringing. My dad, who was a pharmacist, didn't do anything to help run the household. He provided for us financially, but my mother did everything else. I looked at all men, including Dave, as pretty helpless apart from their professions. I was the one taking care of all the details. We didn't see anything wrong with this, because these were the roles we had accepted.

Dave was in so much pain from his broken arm that he really needed me to take care of him. I had to attend to all his needs. He couldn't bathe himself, feed himself, get dressed, or do much of anything else without help. This frustrated him to no end, and on top of all this, he was enduring relentless pain. To make matters worse, he felt discouraged because he couldn't be out on the field with the team as they neared the playoffs. I didn't resent taking care of Dave, but I was exhausted. Because of the stress, Dave's pain, and the sheer chaos of our lives, neither of us got much sleep.

Two weeks after Dave fell from the mound, we had an appointment to meet and interview a writer we were considering to author our book. I was upstairs in our apartment, getting ready to go, out when the phone rang.

I grabbed the phone so it wouldn't disturb Dave. "Hello."

"Jan?"

A familiar and welcome voice came over the line. It was our pastor and friend from our church in Ohio. "Hi, Pastor Bob, how are you?"

"Jan, I'm afraid I have bad news.

"What? What is it?"

"Jan, your father died of a heart attack." He spoke in a somber and consoling tone that should have convinced me that he spoke the truth, but I simply could not believe him.

"You can't be serious."

But he was. He told me that my father had died of a heart attack at work. In the middle of filling a prescription, he turned and dropped dead.

It was like seven years before. I had the same reaction when my mother died. I said the same thing to the pastor that I had said to

Dave when he told me about Mother: "This is a joke, a sick joke. You *are* joking, aren't you?"

The situation was so similar to my mother's death that it did feel like a sick joke. Both had died instantly of a heart attack. They were in Ohio, and I was in California. With each one, I got the call, out of the blue. No one called to say, "They're in the hospital and could possibly die." I received no warning. One minute they were alive, and the next minute they were gone.

The pain that welled up inside of me when my father died included all the pain I had stuffed since my mother died. The pain twisted like a hot knife in my gut.

At first I cried. I cried for my father, for how much I would miss him. And I cried for my mother, whom I still missed. But then I thought, *I don't have time for this right now; I have too much to do and too many people who need me. I'll deal with this later!* So I put it in the back of my mind. Someway, somehow, I put it away and continued doing all the things that needed to be done.

I rushed back to Ohio and took care of my stepmother, took care of my brother, and took care of the funeral arrangements. Even during the funeral I didn't cry much. My relationship wasn't really with my father. My relationship was with my mother. I hadn't fully grieved my mother's death, and I didn't grieve over my dad's death either. I simply maintained. People kept asking me, "Jan, are you okay? I mean, everything that you've had to deal with!" And I replied, "I'm fine . . . I'm fine!" I stuffed my pain so well that I no longer felt it, and I thought it strange when people looked at me with such deep concern. I was fine! What else did they expect? Finally I packed things up and went back to San Francisco.

I was okay as long as I stayed busy. I hated to slow down because then I would feel something hovering over me, an ominous feeling. On Sundays, which were slow days, the pain would begin to creep in, just under the surface of my emotions. But I didn't want to feel any pain, so I stayed busy, effectively stuffing the pain back under the surface again. I loved being busy and thrived on the rush of accomplishing many things every day.

When I came back from Dad's funeral, the Giants were in the playoffs, hoping to make it to the World Series. During the play-offs things really get crazy because a baseball player's wife is also a travel agent, recreation coordinator, and hostess. It seemed like everyone we'd ever known wanted tickets for the World Series. I was in charge of making the arrangements for the tickets, getting the count, getting it to the ball club, making arrangements for hotels, and things of that nature. So I filled up my time, willingly. I kept my pain underground by staying busy and taking care of everyone who was coming for the playoffs.

Even though Dave was restricted to the bench, he was still wearing his uniform and cheering his team on. The time was excit-ing, even if he couldn't be on the mound where he longed to be. For the last game of the playoffs, on October 9, we were up against the Chicago Cubs. Whoever won this game would be going to the World Series.

I knew that if we won, the guys would go wild, jumping all over each other and pounding each other like they do. I didn't want to be a spoilsport, but I wanted Dave to protect his broken arm. Before the game, I pleaded with him, "David, please, what-ever you do, don't go out to the mound for the celebration if we win." He wouldn't promise to stay off the field, but he did promise to wear his brace.

When the final play came, I thought, *Please don't go out there. Please, Dave, don't go out there.* But who do you think was the first one out on the field? My husband, who was then tackled from behind. I was celebrating when someone tapped me on the shoul-der and said, "Look!" I searched the bobbing jumble of men, cheering, slapping, and jumping all over each other. Where was Dave? Then I saw him, holding his arm, excruciating pain written all over his face. He had broken his arm again—this time in a totally different place.

While everyone else was celebrating the Giants' going to the World Series, I was crying and asking God, "Why, Lord? Why now?"

I was so angry with Dave that I could have killed him. But I cried for him too. I cried because he was obviously in so much pain. It never occurred to me that I had plenty of my own pain to cry about; no, I cried for him.

After the second break, Dave was in worse pain than before. He sank into a dark mood, becoming self-absorbed and angry. We had been under considerable pressure, trying to decide which publisher to choose, and this had created conflict with some close friends. He was obviously frustrated at not being able to play. And he wasn't talking. Pain, anger, and frustration were building up within him, and while I tried to help him get past it, I couldn't. I knew something had to give, sooner or later, but I dreaded it.

Before Dave committed his life to Christ, he would occasionally get like this. The pressure would keep building and building until something set him off, sending him into a rage. I hadn't seen him react like that in years, but the familiar signs told me it was only a matter of time. A guy can take only so much. My reaction was to increase my efforts to keep everything around him just so, but too many things were out of my control.

October 17, 1989, a week after the second break, the Giants were in San Francisco for the World Series. Several major events were scheduled for us that day, and one that no one anticipated. We had finally selected a publisher, and we held a press conference in downtown San Francisco that day to announce the upcoming book. Then our family, friends, agents, and representatives from the publishing house went to Candlestick Park to celebrate and watch the World Series game.

While we were at the ballpark, we heard a low rumble. The stands shook, and the ground lurched and rolled. The 1989 San Francisco earthquake hit, and we were terrified. Even after the earth stopped shaking, spectators and players alike stood still, uncertain what to do next. When we looked to the north, we could see that San Francisco was on fire. Some people had little televisions on which we saw reports that the Cypress Expressway had collapsed, along with a portion of the Oakland Bridge.

We tried to call home on the stadium phones, but the lines were down. Our group gathered together and decided to go home to figure out what we should do. Several people had to stop at their hotels and get their belongings before coming over. No one wanted to be alone, so we agreed that everyone would get their things then meet at our house. Dave's parents and I met Dave on the field. Then someone from the Giants' staff escorted us to our car.

The epicenter of the quake was down in Santa Cruz, south of San Francisco, where we were. Oakland, just northeast of us, reported terrible damage and loss of life. Communication lines were down, so we had not heard how much damage was suffered in Santa Cruz or in Foster City, where our children were. I had no way to get in touch with the woman watching Tiffany and Jonathan, and that tormented me.

I wanted nothing more than to race home and make sure the children were safe, but the bumper-to-bumper traffic inched along. A trip that normally took ten to fifteen minutes took two hours.

As the sun set, my heart sank with it. What if my children were in darkness without me there to protect them? I had an eerie feeling traveling down Highway 101 along the Pacific Coast. It was pitch black on either side. Only the ribbons of headlights and the flicker of distant fires penetrated the darkness. All I could think about was the possibility that my children were in total darkness. All I could do was pray.

The block where we lived was on a little island right near the water. When we came within viewing distance, there was only one little patch of land where the homes were illuminated. The small area surrounding my children was the only part of town with electricity. Thank God!

I tried to take care of all of our guests and make them feel comfortable. We had about fourteen people at dinner that night, and some people stayed overnight because their hotels were destroyed or without electricity. At such a very frightening time, we took comfort in being together. When the airport opened again a few days later, our guests flew home.

Dave was in unbelievable pain; the second break seemed worse than the first. So I called Dr. Campbell, who recommended that Dave rest and recuperate. The officials were unsure when the World Series would resume, and the wait was unnerving. I knew I had to take care of Dave, so I went to the general manager and said, "I'm taking Dave home to Ohio. I'm getting him out of here." It was useless to wait for the games to resume since he couldn't play anyway. Besides, I wasn't interested in staying in San Francisco after living through the earthquake.

October 25, I moved the family home to Ohio. The week we got home, we involved ourselves in a stressful situation, trying to help Kristen, a family friend who was suffering from depression. Dave invited her to move in with us and volunteered my help because he thought I was able to take care of everyone and everything. I agreed because we loved Kristen and her parents.

During November, we were writing *Comeback,* the book about Dave's battle with cancer and his return to the major leagues. Dave has a terrible memory, so he used mine. At the same time, Dave went to Cleveland for his regular exam, and we were told that the lump had returned. They didn't know for sure if it was scar tissue or if it was a tumor, so we went to New York for a second opinion. It was definitely a tumor. Dave needed a second operation immediately.

We had a big argument over whether Dave should retire from baseball. I saw his insistence on trying to continue to play as a threat to his health, our family, and maybe to his life. The thought of his retirement made me sad, but I thought the time had come. Dave took longer to make his decision, agonizing over it, especially since the Giants showed enough faith in him to offer him a contract for another year. Finally Dave made the break. He retired from baseball on November 13, 1989.

Christmas season at our house usually starts in early November when I would begin playing Christmas music. But when November came, I wasn't acting like myself. I kept saying to Dave, "What is wrong with me? I couldn't care less about Christmas." I noticed that my normal joy and enthusiasm for life were diminishing. But I didn't take into consideration that my father had been dead less than two months, that we were still writing the book, that I was trying to help Kristen with her problems, and that Dave had just been rediagnosed with cancer. It was no wonder I couldn't enjoy Christmas.

At the same time, my memory was going. I would be in midsentence and forget what I was saying. I would look at people's faces, know who they were, but not have a clue what their names were. It got to be embarrassing. In fact, it got so bad, I even thought I might have a brain tumor.

In December, we finished writing *Comeback*, and Kristen moved out. On January 1, 1990, we went to New York for Dave's second operation. At Memorial Sloan Kettering Hospital, Dave had the remainder of his deltoid removed, a portion of his tricep removed, and then they inserted catheters into his arm and filled the catheters with radium. This treatment, called brachytherapy, worked from the inside out. They had to make sure they killed every last cancer cell, but the radiation also killed the healthy cells. After two weeks of hospitalization, he came back home, but he was very sick.

One thing Dave and I have learned about suffering is that it breaks down one's facade, and what's on the inside comes out. I didn't see Dave's old moodiness throughout his surgery in 1988 and his comeback. But in the fall and winter of 1989–90, when the pain was constant and no relief was in sight, and when he was scheduled for another operation, the facade broke down, and I saw a side of my husband that I didn't like. The frustration, the irritability, the anger, all of that came out. It was always there, building just under the surface, and I could feel the rumble of emotional energy. He was letting loose this intense anger and emotional force, and the kids and I were the ones who felt it.

While the world was praising Dave and raving about what a wonderful person he was, my husband was turning into a monster whose good-guy image I felt bound to protect. I never wanted anyone to see that side of him.

Being a people-pleaser, I couldn't stand the mounting emotional pressure, so I tried to take care of whatever might upset Dave, always trying to pacify him. Proverbs 19:19 says, "A hot-tempered man must pay the penalty; if you rescue him, you will have to do it again." Well, that should have been my memory verse for that season of our lives because again and again I rescued Dave from having to deal with the consequences of his hot temper.

Every morning I got up at 6:00 to get the children off to school. The day was spent nursing Dave, helping him write his book, responding to requests from the media, and making sure the house was spotless. Sometimes I stayed up till 2:00 in the morning because Dave was a stickler when it came to an orderly home, and I wanted to make sure that nothing disturbed him.

On top of all this, the mail that was delivered after Dave's comeback in August—well over ten thousand pieces of it—was still sitting in our garage. Every night I tried to answer some of the letters. We had made public statements that we were going to answer each and every letter because they were so important. Since Dave couldn't answer the letters, I took that on as my responsibility.

To make it through each day, I kept telling myself, "If I can just hold out a little longer, I'll be okay." But I was driving myself nonstop to take care of everyone and everything around me because I thought that was what God wanted me to do.

I believed what everyone said about me, that I was some kind of wonder woman. I had always operated on my own strength. But I was finding that my strength was not sufficient. I couldn't do it all. The load was getting heavier and heavier, and I was getting weaker and weaker.

Dave wasn't the only one in our family who was suffering the effects of intensifying physical stress and emotional pressure. I was, too. However, because Dave's cancer and injuries were so clearly visible and his losses so tangible, we didn't recognize that mine were just as real. I just kept pushing everything—my stress, my physical and emotional needs, my feelings, my losses—down under the surface.

My life was similar to San Francisco before the earthquake. The mounting pressure and conflicting forces that caused the earthquake were all buried deeply underground. On the surface, no one saw any sign of the coming catastrophe, but the pressure was there and had to be released. The same thing was happening within me. If those with understanding had been able to look inside me, they could have predicted that I was due for an emotional earthquake. Something had to give. It was only a matter of time.

Eight

The Invincible Woman Begins to Crumble

*D*uring January and February of 1990, I rarely got more than four or five hours of sleep a night. So much was demanding my attention that I felt I didn't need much sleep. I was always on the alert, never tired, and I attributed this to supernatural strength, not realizing I was living on a constant adrenaline rush. Only when I slowed down, did I feel the ominous black cloud hovering on the horizon. As long as I kept busy, I could keep the cloud at a distance. So our home in Ohio bustled with activity: kids in and out, family dropping by regularly, and constant interaction.

My caretaking covered my family, extended to Kristen, and even to her boyfriend, Paul. Kristen and Paul were both seniors in high school, and both were seriously depressed. In early February, they told Dave and me they were planning to get married right away. Paul had enlisted in the Navy and was apprehensive about going away alone. Dave and I tried to convince them that getting married might not be a good idea, at least not until their lives stabilized a bit. We knew the Lord could help them through these trying times, and then they would be in a far better position to enter into a lifetime commitment. We didn't mean to discourage Paul utterly, but he left our home that night under a dark cloud.

The next evening Dave and I attended a local Youngstown sports banquet where Dave was honored as Man of the Year. When we came home, we had a message from Kristen. Paul had committed suicide.

It was too much. I cried, *I can't do it anymore, God! What are you trying to do to me?*

The suicide was a severe blow, but somehow I regained my strength. I was determined to maintain a positive attitude. Besides, to quote Carly Simon, "I didn't have time for the pain."

For several months, signs of stress overload had been apparent in me, but I didn't recognize them. I had heartburn and severe indigestion every day. I could tell something was going wrong with my body, even though I was still able to keep busy and look happy on the surface. My adrenal system, designed to help me with occasional episodes of danger or special demands, was on alert twenty-four hours a day. We had had so many emergencies, one after the other, that I learned to live continuously in this heightened state of readiness.

About this time, my sister-in-law, Missy, and I attended a church banquet together. I looked across the table to see a strange expression on Missy's face.

"Missy, are you all right?" I asked.

Speechless, she pointed to her mouth and put her hand to her throat. She was choking. I rushed around the table, wrapped my arms around her rib cage, and tried to dislodge the food by force. She still was unable to breathe. I squeezed her as hard as I could, and finally she began coughing and breathing again. This experience terrified both of us. Missy regained her composure, but the fear of not being able to breathe haunted her.

She called me later that week.

"Jan," she said, "something strange is happening to me. Remember how I couldn't breathe when I was choking? The same thing happened to me today when I was driving, but I wasn't eating anything."

"What do you mean, the same thing happened?" I asked.

"I was driving along when suddenly, without any warning, I couldn't breathe. I panicked. My chest hurt terribly. I thought I was having a heart attack or something. I'm scared, Jan. I'm scared."

Missy and I are a lot alike. We have the same personality type, we even look alike, and I've always identified with her in a special way. I hated to hear her going through such pain. I had learned from other family members that since the choking episode, Missy was so afraid of choking again that she refused to eat. I was glad she trusted me enough to confide in me. I saw myself as the one who was going to come in and take care of her, but I didn't know what to make of her strange symptoms or how to help her.

Missy's bouts of fear, accompanied by chest pains and shortness of breath, became so severe she wouldn't leave her house. She just sat in the middle of her living room and cried. She sought psychiatric help and was prescribed antidepressant medication. I didn't like it at all that Missy was seeing a secular psychiatrist. I told her with complete confidence, "Oh, you don't need drugs, Missy. The Lord will help you if you just let him." I called around to find a Christian counselor who dealt with panic disorders, and the counselor assured me that there are times when panic attacks can be helped by medication, along with counseling. I tried to get Missy to go to this Christian counselor. However, her episodes of panic became so debilitating that her doctor recommended she be admitted to the hospital for inpatient treatment.

I did my best with Missy, but when she ended up being hospitalized, I took that as a personal defeat. I tried to encourage Missy, but that didn't seem to be enough. I spent the afternoon with her before she was admitted to the hospital. I took her a devotional book and assured her that the Lord could overcome whatever she was going through. Even though I didn't understand what plagued her and felt uncomfortable with her decision to go into the hospital, I loved Missy and showed my love by being there for her when she needed me.

I trusted that my presence and support would make a positive difference in her life. It did. God used me even in my loving ignorance to encourage Missy. What I did not realize at the time was that God was using Missy's situation to prepare me for what I was about to go through.

Regardless of these disturbing events, I kept pushing myself to keep up with the relentless demands. We had finished Dave's book, and he was about to embark on a book tour. During the last three weeks of March we were scheduled to be in Ohio, Chicago, Washington, D.C., San Francisco, and New York. Not only did I have to schedule a million details in relation to the tour, but I also had to be psyched to fulfill our commitments in each place with each new group of people we were scheduled to meet.

In mid-March, we flew to Chicago, where Dave and I were to speak at Bill Hybels' church, Willow Creek Community Church, one of the fastest growing churches in the country. We were accompanied by our agent, Sealy Yates, and his wife, Susan. As we walked down the long hallway to our hotel room, I shared with Susan my concern over Missy's condition.

"Susan," I said, "have you ever heard of such a thing? I'm so worried about her. I hate to be away when she might need me."

"You mean the panic attacks?" she asked. "Yes, I've heard of them. They aren't uncommon." She hesitated a moment, then continued. "I've experienced them myself. They are not easy to deal with."

I was shocked. Susan was one of the most competent women I knew. I could not imagine her being plagued by fear. "You?" I asked.

"Yes, me and other women you would never suspect. My mother was hospitalized with similar symptoms in the early fifties."

In our room, with Dave and Sealy gone, we continued the conversation.

"Susan, this is strange." I said. "How can it be that I've never heard about panic attacks? I mean, how do you go thirty-four years without ever hearing of this condition if it's so common?"

She explained, "There's a great deal of shame involved. It tends to happen to women who are controllers. Those are the very ones who don't want anyone to know they have a problem. I was having them for a long time before I even shared this with Sealy. I went through the panic attacks and the subsequent depression alone. That's what many people do. They hide the preliminary symptoms of depression or anxiety disorders because they don't want to be labeled as neurotic."

I nodded slowly, trying to understand. But I didn't understand. Not really. Not until I experienced a panic attack firsthand myself.

Ten days later on March 21, 1990, we flew to Washington, D.C. to meet the president. That was where I had the first panic attack.

I tried desperately to find some other explanation for what had happened to me. All my security had been in me, and "me" was falling apart. I was scared to death to think this could be happening. It showed me my frailty, a frailty that was inconceivable before that moment. The thought that I . . . I, Jan Dravecky, was as weak as any other person scared me to death because my personal strength had always been my best and last refuge.

After the panic attack at the J. W. Marriott, I was somehow able to pull myself together without anymore embarrassing episodes, which was a great relief to Dave. We had the pleasure of meeting President Bush. He was very gracious and spoke highly of the courage Dave and I displayed in the face of cancer. And he even made a special point of speaking directly to Tiffany and Jonathan, showing them photos of his grandchildren.

We came back to Ohio for two days, then flew to San Francisco at the end of March. While driving on the freeway with Tiffany and Jonathan in the car, I suddenly felt strange again. Without warning, my heart started pounding erratically. I gripped the steering wheel, barely breathing, dizziness coming over me like a fog. Panicking, I signaled to change lanes, but the cars whizzed past without creating a break for me.

Dear God, please don't let me black out. Please, protect us!

I felt the panic that came with the other physical symptoms but also the terror any mother would feel from putting her children in danger. It was the most horrible and terrifying experience I have known. I don't know how long it lasted, but it was too long. When the symptoms let up, I was able to safely get off the freeway and back to our hotel.

After this episode I was afraid to drive. I didn't realize it at the time, but this was the start of agoraphobia, a fear of going out, which would eventually rob me of my freedom.

I suffered in silence, just as Susan had told me she had done. I dared not tell anyone, not even Dave. I didn't want to be characterized as mentally unstable.

When I came home from San Francisco, I had panic attacks repeatedly throughout one entire day. Still seeking some explanation other than an anxiety disorder, I attributed the severity of these attacks to my menstrual cycle.

But the panic attacks started to happen more and more frequently. By the end of March, when we went to New York to promote Dave's book, I had panic attacks continually throughout the flight. But I learned to control my behavior to keep Dave from noticing. Dave had plenty of his own physical problems to deal with (he hadn't been feeling at all well) so he didn't notice anything unusual in my demeanor.

I was able to maintain my composure during our interview for *Entertainment Tonight*. Then we had dinner with the publicist hired to promote *Comeback*. She told us that Dave was going on the road for the next six weeks. The realization that I was only going to see Dave one day in those six weeks was too much for me. I knew they planned a book tour, but I had no idea it was going to be that demanding.

Over the last several months, I had shifted my focus off myself and onto Dave so entirely that, even though I wouldn't be traveling with him physically, I would be traveling with him emotionally. The thought of Dave's making four or five appearances each day for six weeks was more than I could bear. Also, I realized that Dave was not well, and I had serious reservations about his ability to deal with such a demanding schedule in his poor state of health.

When we went back to our hotel room, I had trouble falling asleep that night, but I didn't have any more panic attacks. The next day, April 6, we were scheduled to appear on *Good Morning, America* and *CBS This Morning*. I knew I needed to get some rest, but my body seemed unable to settle down. The racing motor inside me would not shut off; it was furiously grinding, straining to shift into another gear. When I woke up, I instantly had a sense that I was going to lose control.

Going into the *Good Morning, America* interview, I prayed that Charlie Gibson wouldn't ask me any questions. I prayed silently the entire time they did my makeup and hair. Even when we were on camera while Dave was answering questions, I stared at my hands and repeated Psalm 23 silently as I sat there.

I felt detached from the scene. When Charlie Gibson asked me a question, I smiled and repeated an answer I had given before. No one seemed to notice that I was on edge. He asked me a few more questions. I don't remember what they were, but an answer came out of my mouth. I managed to smile for the cameras. I kept praying, *Lord, just get me through this. I just have a little bit more to go. Just get me through this so I can go home.*

When the interview was over, I felt great relief. We hurried to the studios where Dave would appear on CBS *This Morning*. There I waited in the green room with the publicist, and we watched the program on the television. They were taping Dave's interview to be inserted in the program later. I kept drinking hot tea while I waited, not realizing that the caffeine was revving me up more.

Finally Dave finished taping the interview, and I breathed a huge sigh of relief. Now we could go straight to the airport. I thought I was home free.

As we were preparing to leave, one of the producers came in and said the taping wasn't good. They were going to have to scrap it and do it all over again. That was all I could handle. Even though we would only be delayed an extra fifteen minutes, I was at the end of my rope. That inexplicable fear grabbed me by the throat again, and my heart started pounding wildly.

I said, "David, feel my heart."

He put his hand over my heart, and his eyes showed his alarm. He could feel my heart pounding furiously as though it was coming out of my chest.

"Hey," Dave spoke to someone in the room who worked for the studio. "Hey, we need some help here."

They took me immediately to the nurse's station and made me lie down. Dave held my hand, telling me, "Just take it easy, Jan. You'll be fine. Just take it easy."

I tried to do what he said, but I was totally out of control. My heart rate was unbelievably high, and the nurse was visibly concerned when she took my pulse. For a few minutes, we were all really scared, not knowing what might happen. But as I lay there, trying to breathe slowly, my heart rate came down. I was running a slight fever, but the nurse couldn't diagnose my overall condition. She urged Dave to get me home without delay. So Dave abandoned the interview and rushed me to the airport, where he put me on a plane headed for home.

After this incident, I acknowledged that I had a problem. I had always seen myself as invincible, the one who lived to take care of everyone else. But I had to learn the hard way—through experience—that I was not a god. I could not do it all.

Over the past six months, I'd felt as though I were in a prize fight. Each time I'd get knocked down, I'd say, "Okay, I'm going to be strong." And I would pull myself up by my own power, by my own strength. But I couldn't stand up under the unceasing blows: Dave's cancer, his retirement, his recurrent illness, my parents' deaths, Paul's suicide, our unrelenting schedule. Finally I told God, "I can't do it anymore. I can't do this!"

This is exactly what God wanted me to realize.

God allowed me to exhaust myself at my own game. He didn't want to knock me down and see me out for the count. He simply wanted me to realize that I am not invincible. He wanted me to admit my human frailty and get the help I needed to deal with the overwhelming stresses of my life.

Although I began to give up my notions of invincibility, I still clung to other false beliefs, beliefs that tripped me up, time and again, in the following months. Getting the help I needed turned out to be as long and arduous a journey as finding out that I needed help in the first place.

Nine

Fighting Against Depression

Somehow I survived the flight home without Dave, who continued on his book tour. My friends Bobby and Patty met me at the airport and took me directly to the doctor.

I felt as though I had the flu. My body ached, and I had no energy. The doctor took my temperature and pronounced that I had a low-grade fever. He gave me a blood test and discovered that I was anemic. Hearing these scientific explanations gave me hope that I was just suffering physically from a bad case of the flu. I thought he'd prescribe an antibiotic and I'd be well before Dave came back from his tour.

But then the doctor sat me down and said, "Tell me what's been going on in your life lately. I'm aware of what your husband has been going through, but what about you? What has life been like for Jan Dravecky?"

Somewhat taken aback by his question, I fumbled for an answer. "I've been fine, just taking care of Dave and . . . I'm fine, except for these physical problems. I want to know what's wrong with me. Something is wrong with my body, and I want to know what it is."

"Describe your symptoms and tell me when they began."

I glanced over to my friend Patty for support, then explained about the panic attacks, the dizzy spells, the heart problems. "I'm worried about heart trouble," I concluded. "My parents both died suddenly of heart attacks."

"When did your parents die?" the doctor asked gently.

"My mother in 1982, my father just last fall. Doctor, you need to check my heart. Something is wrong, terribly wrong with my heart; it races. It beats so hard you can see it."

But he steered me back to telling him about my schedule since my first panic attack. I told him about going from Chicago to D.C., then to Ohio, then on to San Francisco for the start of Dave's book tour, then to New York. He stopped me and the expression on his face made me worry that he might have a coronary.

"No wonder you're having these symptoms!" he exclaimed.

"What is it? Is it my heart? It's too much for my heart, right?" I anxiously awaited his diagnosis. Maybe it was a heart condition that could be treated before it was too late.

"My dear, it's too much for you, period. You are suffering from depression. These physical symptoms are part of the package."

"What? You said yourself that I have a fever. This feels like the flu, and what about my heart? There is something really wrong with my heart." Again, I looked to Patty for support; her raised eyebrows told me she shared my skepticism. This gave me courage to state my case more firmly. "There is something wrong with me, and you'd better find out what is wrong. It is not depression! I don't feel depressed."

"Jan, try to calm down. Let me explain it to you. I know you are experiencing physical problems; that's part of the pattern. Depression is more than just feeling blue. Your brain is a sensitive part of your body. It's affected by stress as much as any other organ. Whenever a person experiences a serious loss, unwelcome changes, stresses of one form or another, your body and mind are affected. Stress takes its toll on your immune system, making you more vulnerable to physical illness—"

"That's what I'm trying to tell you," I interrupted. "There is something wrong with my body, and it scares me. I don't want to die of a heart attack while people sit around talking about psychological problems."

"Depression is a condition that affects your whole body," the doctor explained patiently. "It's not just psychological or emotional. Depression can occur when the biochemical balance in your brain is disturbed by too much stress. This imbalance triggers the other symptoms in your body. I see this more and more these days. One out of four women will experience clinical depression in her lifetime, and this has a lot to do with the tremendous demands on women today. Dark emotions are only one of many symptoms of depression; it is as much physical as it is emotional."

I still wasn't convinced. He could sense as much and changed his approach. "My dear, you've been through so much. . . . I'm amazed you're doing as well as you are. But you must face what is happening to you and get appropriate help for your depression." The doctor looked at me with compassion. I'm sure he believed what he was saying, but he didn't know me.

"Sir, I don't mean to be rude," I said, "but I am a Christian, and Christians don't get depressed. I have the hope of Jesus in my heart, that's why I do not feel depressed even though we've been through so much. How can you say it's depression? Is that all you doctors know how to diagnose? There is something wrong with me, and you need to find out what it is." I didn't feel depressed; I felt downright impatient.

I guess he realized I was not going to accept his diagnosis. He told me that I needed rest, that was all. I needed rest! Great! I almost died, and he tells me to go home and rest.

As I lay in bed that night, I could visibly see my heart pounding out of my chest. Waves and waves of tingling swept through my body. It was the most horrible feeling, suffering alone, afraid I was about to die with no one to help me. I could not get out of bed that night. I lay as still as I could, fear rising in me. Then the panic came over me again, and I thought I was dying. I couldn't breathe, couldn't even call out to anyone. My heart raced erratically, sweat covered me, and something choked off my breath. When this episode finally subsided, I determined to go back to the doctor and convince him to help me. This was something real, not just in my mind.

I called the doctor Saturday morning and said, "Please help me. Something is really wrong with me." He told me to come into the office. This time he checked my heart, blood pressure, and temperature again. All seemed normal. He didn't try to convince me that I was depressed this time. He just gave me a prescription for Pamalar, a type of antidepressant, and said, "You need rest!" That was on Saturday.

On the Pamalar, I could not raise my head off the pillow. I went from operating at a frenetic pace to being totally incapacitated, flat on my back. My heart palpitations seemed to go from bad to worse. The waves of tingling continued to torment me; but now I could not move. I could not get out of bed.

As I lay there, I felt tremendous guilt, guilt that I could not take care of my own children, guilt for going on medication instead of trusting God to conquer this thing, guilt that Dave's parents had to help out, guilt, guilt, guilt! People from church were always nearby, but they just made me feel more guilty. They would suggest that I needed to pray more and read my Bible more. Those things were fine, but I wasn't able. I couldn't concentrate well enough to read, and prayer seemed impossible. They, too, didn't seem to understand that this wasn't just spiritual or psychological; this was physical.

By Tuesday morning, I was hysterical. I called the doctor back and said, "Please, doctor, please help me!" He scheduled an appointment for me to come in the next day.

Patty drove me to the doctor's office on Wednesday because I couldn't drive myself. I couldn't even hold up my head. The doctor began with a ten-question test*:

"Jan, have you cried a lot lately?"

I said, "Yes, I've cried every day."

"Have you had disturbances in your regular sleep patterns?"

"Yes, but how can I be expected to sleep when my body is going crazy?"

"Have you lost interest and pleasure in activities you formerly enjoyed?"

"Yes, but I'm sick."

"Have you experienced a significant loss of energy, feeling fatigued?" He checked that one off without waiting for my answer. I was crumpled in my chair, my head resting on my shoulder. But I blamed the medication for that.

"Do you have feelings of worthlessness?" he asked, looking genuinely concerned.

"Well, yes, but I can't take care of my own children. I mean, I'm not worth much to anyone in this condition. That doesn't mean I'm depressed."

"Do you have an inability to concentrate, think, or make clear decisions?"

"Yes." Obviously he was trying to make a point. I was too tired to argue.

---

*The questions appearing here are adapted from the Mental Illness Awareness Guide, revised in 1994 by the American Psychiatric Association. I do not recall if these are the exact questions I was asked at the time, but they are similar. These are the appropriate questions one should use to determine whether someone may be suffering from depression. A person who experiences four or more of these symptoms for more than two weeks should seek professional help.

"Do you have unusual physical symptoms like headaches, stomachaches, or severe heartburn?"

"Yes."

"Do you have persistent feelings of inappropriate guilt?"

"Well, yes; but I think it's appropriate. I should be able to take care of my children. I do feel terribly guilty."

"Do you have persistent feelings of hopelessness, sadness, and grief that overwhelms you, accompanied by waking at least two hours earlier than usual?"

"Doctor, I told you. I have the hope of Jesus. I'm only crying because . . . because no one will help me, and I'm afraid I'm going to die. But I do wake up earlier than usual. I wake up with a start, it's awful. I wake up feeling terrible, in my body, not my mind."

"Jan, do you have disturbed thinking? Are you making decisions based on beliefs that are not based on reality?" I could see in his eyes what he thought the answer to this question was; he thought I was cracked! Maybe I was! I was so unsure of myself, and all I wanted was help. I began to cry.

"Doctor, I don't know what's wrong with me. I just know I need help. Please help me."

He said emphatically, "Jan, you're depressed."

"How can you tell I'm depressed from a ten-question quiz? I don't feel depressed! My body's falling apart, but emotionally I don't feel depressed!"

He said, "You are suffering from depression. It may be a mild case, but you are suffering from depression. You need to see a psychiatrist. I can't help you. If this is depression, a psychiatrist will be able to give you a better diagnosis and prescribe the appropriate medication."

Patty's eyes grew wide, as though she was trying to warn me without saying anything in front of the doctor. We both shared a strong skepticism toward secular psychiatry. However, I took the doctor's advice and made an appointment with a psychiatrist.

When we got home, Patty called Dave and told him, "She's really bad! You need to get back home."

Dave insisted on coming home to me, interrupting the book tour at great expense and much to the chagrin of everybody involved. This just added to my sense of guilt.

That afternoon as I rode with Patty to the psychiatrist, I could sense her ambivalence. She obviously didn't want to be an accomplice to something she saw as being totally against the Lord, that is, going to a psychiatrist; but she didn't want to abandon me either. I knew my in-laws would be totally upset that I was going to a psychiatrist, so I had no choice but to rely on my closest friend. However, that ride was somewhat less than friendly.

"Jan," she began, "I don't know if you're doing the right thing, going to the world." Patty was a member of our church. The pastor taught us that Jesus and the Bible were the only source of help needed to deal with emotional and spiritual problems.

I tried to pick up my head to look at her but couldn't manage it. I turned toward her, "Patty, please don't be mad at me. I'm not going to let him do anything weird. I just want to get some help. After all, maybe this *is* something stress-related." She didn't talk for a few moments.

"Jan, what if it is spiritual?" she said finally. "God only knows what kind of spiritual forces you may be opening the door to by going to someone who doesn't know the Lord. How can you go to the world? It's dangerous."

I didn't say anything more, and neither did she. We rode in an awkward silence. I closed my eyes.

Walking into that psychiatrist's office felt like walking into Satan's den. I don't know if I'd been influenced by Patty's comments or if it was real, but I had a sense of being surrounded by demonic influences. The decor was black and gray. Can you imagine a psychiatrist's waiting room being black and gray? His office was dark brown, not exactly what I would call cheery!

Patty gave me a look that said, "I told you so!"

A female therapist came into the office where Patty and I were waiting. She gave me a written evaluation with many questions. When I finished that, she gave me a music tape and told me to listen to the music and empty my mind. Emptying my mind was the last thing I was about to do; I knew the danger of emptying my mind and filling it with anything but the truth of God's Word. So I remained on guard.

The psychiatrist came in and looked over my chart and notes from his assistant, but he didn't tell me anything. Finally he asked me, "How long have you been on the Pamalar?"

"Five days."

"Hmm . . . we're going to take you off that. I don't think it's what you need." He didn't volunteer why he took me off the Pamalar, nor did he prescribe a new medication. With no further explanation and with no future appointment planned, I left his office more confused than when I came.

By the time Dave got home that night, I couldn't function at all. I was lying in bed when he came in, and I couldn't get up. He looked worried and started asking questions at lightning speed. He wanted to know what they did to me. His worry and frustration over not being able to fix this problem came across as anger, but I knew Dave well enough not to let that bother me.

I could only imagine the shock Dave must have felt when he saw me. Here was his wife . . . Wonder Woman . . . Wonder Christian . . . lying flat on her back in bed, unable to lift her head. If you had asked Dave, he would have told you I was more powerful than a locomotive and could jump tall buildings in a single bound.

Besides that, I could see in his eyes that he couldn't comprehend why I had collapsed when he was the one who had been through everything—the cancer, the surgery, the pain, as well as the long work of physical therapy. He didn't realize I had gone through everything with him, and the stress was taking its toll.

He left the room, probably to talk with Patty and his parents. Then he came back in and pronounced, "You will not go back to that psychiatrist!"

That night, I had panic attacks all night long. I couldn't sleep, but Dave lay next to me, snoring. I looked at him, taking comfort in his presence and thinking of all he had been through. I didn't want to wake him up because he needed his rest. But a couple of times I was so sure I was in danger and felt so scared that I did wake him up.

At 6:30 in the morning I woke Dave again, in a panic. He got up and called the psychiatrist's exchange. I heard him on the phone: "She's losing it! I want to know what is going on and what I can do to help her. Something is wrong; this is not like Jan at all."

He listened for a moment, then hung up. "The psychiatrist prescribed an antianxiety drug," he told me, avoiding my eyes. "I'll go get it." And he left.

I could sense his hesitation. He didn't know if he was helping me or hurting me. He just had to do something, and this was what we were told to do.

Then Dave got on the phone and started calling people we trusted. He called Jeff Ferrar, who had been our pastor in San Francisco. Jeff had just gone through a deep depression. He said, "Dave, call my counselor. You need to check your priorities. You need to stay home and get her a good Christian psychologist. You don't want her going to a secular psychiatrist, but you need to take her for counseling. You need to support her; that means you need to cancel that book tour."

So Dave called Jeff's counselor in San Francisco and described everything again. The counselor told Dave, "What you're describing to me is a stress reaction. She's burned-out!" He didn't use the word *depression*. Dave and I could accept that explanation because we still thought you had to be in a black mood to be depressed.

When Dave told me he had postponed the book tour, I was disturbed.

"Oh, Dave, I don't want you to have to ruin your book tour because of me."

"It's done," he said firmly.

"But what about—"

"Look, Jan, I'm your husband. God gave me a responsibility to take care of you, and that's what I intend to do. Look at you; you can't even lift your head off the pillow. I'm supposed to go jetting all over the country talking about my comeback? No way."

"But, David—"

He wouldn't let me finish. "Look at me; I'm not well either. I feel awful. Look at my arm." He lifted his sleeve to expose what was left of his arm. It had been four months since January, when they had done the surgery and radiation therapy, and the skin had not grown back over the bone. The flesh was laid open, covered with yellow and green layers of pus. You could stick your finger in and touch his bone. The flesh was starting to rot, it smelled, and it seeped all the time.

I still felt guilty for making him cancel his tour, but I conceded.

Dave found me a Christian psychologist and took me there for help. I sat slumped in the chair in the counselor's office, with my head leaning against the armrest.

"So," the counselor began in a soothing voice, "why don't you tell me what the problem is and what I can do to help you?"

I didn't have the energy to do anything, so Dave spoke up for me, "Look at her. She can't drive. She can't do anything. This isn't like her. She's practically bedridden."

"Jan," the counselor addressed me directly. "Tell me what you've been through. Tell me everything."

So once again I told our story, starting with Dave's cancer, then my dad's death, which led me to my mother's death, my heart problems, the panic attacks, our crazy schedule, trying to take care of everyone, the mountains of mail. It seemed to take hours, but I told him everything that had happened to me, sobbing uncontrollably as I did so.

Dave had never seen me like this. He certainly had never heard me feeling sorry for myself. I used to pride myself on carrying everyone else's burdens. I didn't try to hide my own burdens; I just never acknowledged them to myself or anyone else. Dave's concern was visible by the troubled expression on his face.

The counselor responded, "My child, no wonder you're depressed! You've experienced so much loss in your life, and you haven't acknowledged any of it. The pain that you've experienced . . . what have you done with it? You haven't grieved the death of your father. More so, I don't even think you've grieved the death of your mother. You need to go back and grieve."

The session really upset me. It made me look at my losses, and worse (to my way of thinking at the time), to *feel* them. And one thing I did not want was any more pain.

I went home and called a friend from church and told her all about it. She must have told the pastor because he called and said, "Jan, I heard what that counselor told you. He's wrong. You do not need to look back! I don't care if he calls himself a Christian or not. Telling you to look back is wrong. It's so humanistic. If God gave you the grace to go through your father's death without falling apart, you don't need to look back! You just need to trust God for the grace to face today. Trust me. I'm your counselor."

Dave was listening, but I couldn't tell if he was being swayed by our pastor.

The pastor continued, "You don't need to look back. Philippians 3:13 and 14 says, 'Brothers, I do not consider myself yet to have taken hold of it. But one thing I do: Forgetting what is behind and straining toward what is ahead, I press on toward the goal to win the prize.' You see, Jan, Scripture says you are not to look back, but to strain to look toward what is ahead."

Despite my pastor's words, I went back to the Christian psychologist again. And again it upset me. This time he had me talk about my mom. I missed my mom so much, especially since my collapse.

I told the counselor about a time recently when I was stretched out on the couch, and Dave's mom was nearby. She heard me give a deep sigh. "Jan, what's wrong, honey?" she asked.

I told her, "I just wish it would all go back to normal. I wish I was okay again."

She came over and started to rub my back. It felt so good, but I began to cry uncontrollably.

Just telling the doctor about this incident brought on the tears. All I could think about was how much I missed my mom. How I wished I could look up and see my mom there. But she wasn't there for me anymore, and as much as everyone was trying, nothing could ever fill that void.

The counselor looked into my eyes and asked, "You've been looking for someone to lean on, and you have no one to lean on, do you?"

As though he had pulled out a plug, and all the sorrow stored away since my mother died came flooding out. I was sobbing. "I have no one! I have no one that I can lean on! Everybody leans on me, but there is no one I can lean on!"

"Have you looked for that someone since your mother died?"

"No, I don't want to lean on anyone! No one!" I realized he was right. Since my mother had died, I had not allowed myself to lean on anyone. The truth was, I never wanted to need anyone ever again the way I had needed her. This was my protection from being hurt.

"What about Dave? Surely you can lean on your husband, can't you?

"I could, but there's a danger. I might . . . I might lose David. I don't ever want to need anyone—including him."

After that session, Dave and I felt more comfortable with what the pastor had told us. Maybe we should leave the past alone; after all, thinking about it only seemed to bring more pain. At that time I didn't understand that letting the pain out was an upsetting but necessary part of getting free from depression. Instead, I believed I was not really depressed but that these people were making me depressed. I blamed the ones who brought the pain to the surface for my growing emotional pain.

I went to the counselor without Dave for my regular appointment because Dave was out of town. That session, on April 30, turned out to be my last. When Dave called, I explained what had happened.

"Dave, it was so weird. While I was in there seeing him, he brought in this other man that he was training. Do you know what the man asked me? Questions about sex. This man I've never met before looked at me and said, 'Tell me, you're married to a ballplayer. Do you think that part of your condition is related to the fact that you don't trust your husband?'"

Dave was livid. "He said what?"

"Wait, there's more. He asked me, 'How are you two sexually? Do you fear that your husband had a sexual relationship without you?' All his questions revolved around sex!"

"So what did you tell him?"

"Oh, I was angry. I didn't answer him! At least I had enough of my faculties about me to know he was not asking me the right questions. This obviously had nothing to do with anything. In all my other sessions, nobody had ever asked me about sex except to examine whether I was sexually molested when I was young."

"This was the trainee, right? What did the counselor do?" Dave asked. "Did he go along with the guy?"

"No, he seemed to realize the guy was way off-base. He just tried to steer the session in a different direction. The one thing the counselor focused on is that I have to be careful not to be under any more stress."

After some more discussion, Dave and I made a decision that I was sure the counselor would not like. We decided these counseling sessions were one of the major causes of stress in my life and that I wasn't depressed, just stressed out. We thought that if I could just rest and focus on the Lord, I would eventually get better.

At that time, I went to another doctor recommended by a friend. Dr. McGowen, who had gone through depression just a year before, recognized my controlling behavior, physical symptoms, and emotional condition. He took one look at me and said, "You're going through depression." Then he listened to my heart and said, "But I think you also have mitral valve prolapse. That is when one of the valves in your heart doesn't close correctly. This condition is aggravated by stress. When the mitral valve doesn't close correctly, it sounds like an extra heartbeat. Prolonged stress causes the heart to go into arrhythmia. That is what happens when your heart begins to race and you go into a panic attack."

So he sent me for a test—an echocardiogram—and sure enough, I had a very pronounced mitral valve prolapse. I was so relieved that someone had finally identified the physical problem. So much of the panic I felt came from the fear over what was happening to me when my heart went crazy.

They were able to bring my panic attacks under control with a medication called a beta blocker, which stops adrenaline from getting to the heart. Anytime I would have an adrenaline rush that would normally cause my heart to go berserk, the medication stopped it. I still had the tingling sensations; I still had shortness of breath, but I didn't have the heart palpitations.

My doctor, too, was pleased with the results. "No wonder your heart went crazy when you were on Pamalar," he said. "That particular medication aggravated your heart condition." Then he looked me straight in the eye and said gently, "But, Jan, you're still suffering from depression. You should either go on antidepressant medication, get counseling, or both."

"Oh, no," I insisted. "I'm going to be fine. I'm not going to play around with more medications. I'm going to get my rest, and I'll get strong. The Christian psychologist told me that if I got six weeks of complete bed rest, maybe I would heal and not need to go on any antidepressants. I appreciate your concern, Dr. McGowen, but I'll just take the bed rest."

I had had of enough doctors and psychiatrists and psychologists. I had had enough of medication. I was going to bed. All I needed—all I wanted—was some rest.

Ten

Bed Rest

*T*hat same day I put myself to bed. I told Dr. McGowen I planned to get well by taking complete bed rest for six weeks, as the Christian counselor had suggested. I had had such negative experiences with all the psychiatrists and psychologists that I didn't want to trust any of them, not even Dr. McGowen. I was determined to take care of myself by resting, reflecting on God's Word, and prayer.

I was thankful that my bedroom was a cheerful place, decorated with beautiful floral wallpaper. I positioned myself in bed with my Bible and stacks of spiritually uplifting books on my bedside table.

It was the first of May. The sun shone into the room, bringing warmth and light I did not feel inside. I was even able to open my windows and let the fresh spring air in. I could hear the birds singing outside. Spring is my favorite season. Oh! How I longed to be outside, feel the sun on my face, and smell the flowers blooming outside my window, but I couldn't. I didn't have the energy. Outside there appeared to be so much life; inside my bedroom I felt as though I was dying. But springtime brings with it the hope

of new life, rebirth, and resurrection. Even though I felt like I was
dying, I clung to the hope that new life would follow if I could only
get enough rest.

As I lay there for hours on end, I wondered what in the world
had happened to me. I had always had so much energy and zeal for
life. Now, making it to the bathroom was a major accomplishment.
The only way I could gather the strength to make it from my bed
to the shower was to sing praise songs to God.

To anyone looking at me from the outside, it may have
appeared that I was a broken woman. I was barely able to lift my
head off the pillow, yet I could not sleep. I didn't eat, because I had
no appetite.

One day when my stepmom came to watch Tiffany and
Jonathan and help take care of me, I overheard her telling a friend,
in hushed tones, "She's having a nervous breakdown!"

In old-fashioned terms, I guess she was right.

I still wanted desperately to be able to take care of my children,
but I thought that if I rested as I was told, I would regain my
strength and be able to take care of them even sooner. In this way,
I consoled myself that it was okay to stay in bed. Tiffany and
Jonathan were surrounded by a large and loving family who com-
pensated for the love and care I was unable to give them. Relatives
took turns relieving me of responsibilities and keeping house, so
my family was taken care of, even though I couldn't do anything.

My biggest emotional problem while resting was managing the
guilt I felt for being in bed while my family needed me. Lying in
bed, with no distractions (since there was no TV in the room) gave
me time to think of everything I should be doing, but couldn't.
From time to time I could hear Tiffany and Jonathan, then eight
and five, playing in the other room. Eventually, I would hear them
arguing. The argument would escalate until, sure enough, within
seconds I would hear the patter of little feet headed for my bedroom. One or both would burst into my room, tattling on each

other. They both knew, as I did, that even in my weakened state, Mother was still the peacemaker. I would help them settle the issue at hand, and then they'd run off to continue their play. Oh, how I wished I could be more of a mother to them at this time.

Hour after hour, day after day, I lay in bed, staring at the ceiling, with my Bible open beside me and several Christian books stacked on my bedside table. I took comfort in passages of Scripture that affirmed my decision to stay in bed, passages like Psalm 63:6–8.

> On my bed I remember you;
> I think of you through the watches of the night.
> Because you are my help.
> I sing in the shadow of your wings.
> My soul clings to you;
> your right hand upholds me.

During the long watches of the night, when sleep would not come, I comforted myself with the stories of great saints like Elijah, who also experienced depression immediately following great spiritual victories. He even asked God to take his life. *Well,* I thought with a small measure of relief, *at least I'm not that far gone.*

I was not suicidal, but whenever I heard about someone who had committed suicide, I went bonkers. It scared me, not because I wanted to die, but because I feared that I was losing my mind and might do something dangerous. These fears drove me to read John 10:27–29 every day: "My sheep listen to my voice; I know them, and they follow me. I give them eternal life, and they shall never perish; no one can snatch them out of my hand. My Father, who has given them to me is greater than all; no one can snatch them out of my Father's hand." These verses reassured me that no one— not me, nor Satan—could take me out of God's care.

During the long days in bed, I struggled spiritually. I did not feel God or sense him in any way, even when I tried to recount the "monuments" in our lives, the times when God had been with us and done great things. Over and over again I tried to reassure myself that God had been real to me at one time and that he had not forsaken us. I wrestled with questions about why God would let such terrible things happen to us. Our struggle was so different from what I had been led to believe the Christian life would be, and I was overwhelmed with confusion. I searched the Scripture, trying to make sense of our suffering. Finally I found these words in Hebrews 12:7–11, and they gave me a new perspective from which to view what was happening.

> Endure all hardship as discipline; God is treating you as sons. For what son is not disciplined by his father? If you are not disciplined, (and everyone undergoes discipline), then you are illegitimate children and not true sons. Moreover, we have all had human fathers who disciplined us and we respected them for it. How much more should we submit to the Father of our spirits and live! Our fathers disciplined us for a little while as they thought best, but God disciplines us for our good, that we may share in his holiness. No discipline seems pleasant at the time, but painful. Later on, however, it produces a harvest of righteousness and peace for those who are trained by it.

Even though I could not sense God, I still clung to his Word as truth. I underlined this passage and determined that I would endure all our hardships as discipline. I would submit to my Father in heaven and live, even though God seemed nowhere to be found.

I did not want to lose my God. So I took great comfort in John 6:39 where Jesus says, "And this is the will of him who sent me, that I shall lose none of all that he has given me, but raise them up at the last day."

I was assured of my salvation, but because I was weak, doubts assailed me as I lay there. At those times, it was as though Satan came in and whispered, "Did you really trust Christ? Are you really saved?"

I became obsessed with reassuring myself that God would keep me because I was afraid that I couldn't keep my own faith strong. I clung to verses like Romans 8:38–39: "For I am convinced that neither death nor life, neither angels nor demons, neither the present nor the future, nor any powers, neither height nor depth, nor anything else in all creation, will be able to separate us from the love of God that is in Christ Jesus our Lord."

Many days all I could do was lay in bed and cry, repeating those verses over and over to reassure myself.

Staying in bed was most difficult for me when Dave and our friends were still out there going places. I would have loved to go with them, but couldn't. One such event was a concert of the Christian rock band, Petra. We had been associated with a Petra concert back in the fall of 1989 as a thank-you to San Francisco, and had developed a friendly relationship with the band members. Now they were scheduled to do a concert in Akron on May 3, 1990, near our home. Dave invited them to our house for a dessert reception after the concert.

Although I had put myself to bed, I ordered the food and got up to set the table. But I quickly felt myself tire, and I didn't even have the energy to finish setting the table. I had to go back to bed while Dave went to the concert without me.

After the concert, I heard their tour bus pull up outside our house. I gathered my strength, and went downstairs to greet them. But again, I did not have enough energy to stay and chat. I went back up to bed, even though I longed to play hostess. I could hear the party going on as I lay upstairs alone.

The band members were worried about me; I could tell from the looks on their faces. The last time they had seen me, just six months earlier, I had looked healthy; now I weighed twenty pounds less and looked sickly and exhausted.

I felt such shame. I was ashamed that Dave was down there alone, having to make excuses for me. And I knew that he was confused and ashamed, too.

Right after the Petra concert, Dave had to go to New York for a checkup on his arm. The last time I had seen the Christian counselor, he made it clear to me that I could not take one more ounce of stress. I was only one week into my self-imposed rest, so I stayed home in bed and prayed that all would be well with Dave. He was hoping the doctor would give him the go-ahead to resume his book tour.

When Dave called me at home and told me he wanted to put Dr. Brennan on the line, I braced myself.

Dr. Brennan said, "Jan, Dave is going to require another surgery."

I said, "What?"

In the back of my mind, I could hear the counselor's voice saying, "Jan, you can't handle one more ounce of stress."

I told Dr. Brennan, "But what about his book tour?"

Dr. Brennan took a firm tone of voice with me, like a father scolding a child. "Young lady, we're talking about your husband's life, not some dumb book tour! My job is to make sure he is here to go on a book tour next year, not next week."

His life? What did he mean, "We're talking about your husband's life"? The doctors had never told us Dave's life was in danger! We had always looked at everything as precautionary so Dave's life wouldn't be endangered. Now it hit me for the first time. Dave still had cancer, and he could die. The reality of that threat blasted through my numbness, shaking me to the core.

I concluded the conversation in a dazed state of mind. I got all the details down and told Dave I would come to New York, somehow. It was still a bright spring day, but inside my heart the lights had gone out. The birds were still singing outside my window, but now their joyful chirping seemed a mockery. Ha! No more stress!

Complete bed rest! Ha! How could I shield myself from stress when God kept knocking me down every time I tried to get up?

My thoughts raced. How was I going to get to New York when I could barely get to the bathroom? It seemed I had no one ... no one to take care of me. I had taken care of everyone else until I collapsed, but now that I was falling apart, it felt like no one was there to take care of me.

Burying my face in my hands, I cried. But no one heard my sobs. My mother was dead, my father was dead, and Dave was far away, his life in danger. If God was there, as he said, why was he letting all these terrible things happen to us? I felt utterly alone. If I hadn't been depressed before, I sure was now.

I asked Dave's parents, Frank and Donna, to stay at our house in Ohio and take care of the children. I knew they wanted to go to New York to be with Dave, but I needed to know my children would be in good hands. They reluctantly agreed to stay with Tiffany and Jonathan. Meanwhile, our friends Bobby and Patty agreed to go with me to New York to take care of me.

On May 6, 1990, we were in New York when Dave checked into the hospital. I looked horrendous and felt as bad as I looked. I was so dizzy and weak I couldn't sit up. The first day Dave was in the hospital, before his operation, I lay in his bed because I couldn't hold up my head, and he sat in the bedside chair. The San Francisco Giants were in New York playing the Mets. So several of Dave's former teammates came over to see him before his operation. They were shocked to come in and find me in the hospital bed, looking far worse than the man who had cancer. They were very kind to both of us and politely concerned. I know they must have been thinking, *What in the world happened to Jan? She looks terrible.* But no one said anything.

The medical staff members were worried about me as well. They must have seen other family members like me, people whose lives were falling apart from the stress of dealing with cancer. So

I'm sure that they knew the warning signs and could tell I was going through a breakdown.

The operation was supposed to be plastic surgery to repair the hole in Dave's arm, but it ended up being much more. While they were in there doing their scraping, they confirmed that the tumor had returned. They had to cut out the tumor and the muscle all around it. Then no muscle was left to protect his bone, which was still healing from both breaks. So they decided to remove eighteen inches of the long muscle from Dave's back and wrap it around the bone in his upper arm to provide protection. Then they had to take skin off his leg to cover the muscle they wrapped around his arm. It looked deformed, a patchwork; it looked gross, but it did the job. What they didn't know was whether the tumor had entered the bone, and they were trying to decide if they needed to replace the bone.

When Dave came out of surgery, he was weak and discouraged. I was getting worse, but I would sit at the bedside, as best I could. Bobby and Patty would go out and get my meals and try to prop me up, until it became obvious to everyone that I really did require complete bed rest. After five days, I agreed to go home, even though it broke my heart to leave Dave alone. Feeling like a failure, I flew home with Bobby and Patty.

Frank and Donna decided to move in with us. It was obvious to everyone that I needed help and that I certainly couldn't take care of Dave or the children. They were so good to us. Yet even when I finally had someone willing to care for me, I had a hard time receiving their love and care because I felt as if I was a disappointment and embarrassment to them. After all, I was the second of their daughters-in-law to have a breakdown.

Dave remained in the hospital another week after I came home. He called our agent, Sealy Yates, who flew from California to stay with him and bring him home on May 18.

Two days after Dave returned home from New York, I got a call from my cousin, Mark, the oncologist. He had bad news. The biopsy reports were back from the surgery, confirming that more tumor existed. Then he told me that Dave and I should prepare ourselves; in his opinion it was only a matter of time before Dave would lose his arm.

I started crying again. I couldn't take much more. I just couldn't. I closed my drapes, pulled the covers up over my head, and sobbed. I stayed in bed, hour after hour, day after day, for the next three weeks, but I had lost any hopes that bed rest could cure me. I still turned to the books on my bedside table, but with a heavy heart as if scavenging for scraps of hope I did not really expect to find. My heart connected with King David, especially the dark passages he wrote in the psalms, like this one in Psalm 42:9–11:

> I say to God my Rock,
>   "Why have you forgotten me?"
> Why must I go about mourning,
>   oppressed by the enemy?"
> My bones suffer mortal agony
>   as my foes taunt me,
> saying to me all day long,
>   "Where is your God?"
> Why are you so downcast, O my soul?
>   Why so disturbed within me?
> Put your hope in God,
>   for I will yet praise him,
>   my Savior and my God.

I wasn't sure if I had the strength to put my hope in God anymore. I knew that God came through for King David, but I thought, *That was someone in the Bible—could God possibly be working in my life in the same way? I'm only Jan Dravecky. Who am I? Would God really be my Savior too?* I wasn't sure if God would save me from this darkness or not, but I underlined the passage anyway.

I was starting to experience moments of utter darkness, dark days where I would feel a black fog come over everything in my life.

Nothing looked good; life had lost all joy. As I lay there in one of these black emotional fogs with strange thoughts floating around in my mind, I looked up at the sky through the crack in my bedroom curtains, and the sky did not seem real to me. I lifted my hands before my face, and I didn't even feel them. I couldn't feel God's presence, and I couldn't even remember what it felt like to believe in him. Nor could I remember what joy felt like.

I had been in bed for a solid month, and staying in bed obviously wasn't helping. It drove me nuts; all it did was make me feel guilty, and the guilt was making me more and more depressed. I was grasping at straws. Since staying in bed wasn't helping, I thought maybe I would be better off to get up and try to get on with life.

I saw no light; I felt no hope; I had absolutely no strength left in myself. *What do you want from me, God?* I asked him in desperation. *What do you want?*

Eleven

Losing My Grip

I made myself get out of bed, although I was still very weak. I sat at my dining room table, sipping a cup of tea and gazing out the window at the flowers in my backyard garden. I sat there wishing life could go back to the way it used to be. The leaves on tree were swaying in the breeze and shimmering in the sunlight. Their lovely spring green was deepening into a shade that heralds the coming of summer. I watched a sparrow hopping from branch to branch, stopping to chirp as if tuning the notes of his song. He seemed to sing a song of joy, a song I couldn't yet sing; but his bright song reminded me that joy was still alive somewhere. For that, I was grateful.

At that moment, an impression came to me unbidden. It was this: *All your life, Jan you have tried to remove pain and create happiness by manipulating people and circumstances. It has been like a juggling act for you. But, Jan, it is not up to you. You need to let go. If you let go, I'm going to show you a joy you've never known.*

I knew this came from God, not me, because it was opposed to anything I would have told myself. I kept telling myself, "*Hold on, just hold on!*" I didn't even know what it meant to let go!

Then I recalled a passage I had underlined in Oswald Chamber's devotional book *My Utmost for His Highest* while I was still confined to bed. I found the book and the underlined passage. It read:

> To become one with Jesus Christ, a person must be willing not only to give up sin, but also surrender his whole way of looking at things. Being born again by the Spirit of God means that we must first be willing to let go before we can grasp something else.... Are we willing to surrender our grasp on all that we possess, our desires, and everything else in our lives? Are we ready to be identified with the death of Jesus Christ?
>
> We will suffer a sharp and painful disillusionment before we fully surrender.... If you are faced with the question of whether or not to surrender, make a determination to go on through the crises, surrendering all that you have and all that you are to Him. And God will then equip you to do all that He requires.[1]

I was willing to let go, even though that seemed backward to me. *Lord, I've been doing all I can not to lose my grip, now you're telling me to let go? Well, okay. I'm willing, but you will have to show me how.*

Then again, maybe letting go was inevitable; I seemed to be losing my grip anyway. In fact, it seemed that the harder I tried to hold on to the old life we used to know, the more God kept prying my fingers loose.

God seemed to be allowing Dave's pitching arm and my mind to be destroyed simultaneously, hitting both of our greatest strengths at the same time. That summer, Dave had to go through eight weeks of external radiation in an attempt to save his arm. His arm blistered, and a staph infection set in. Dave's strength, identity, and ability to make a living were wrapped up in his pitching arm. My strength, self-confidence, and career depended on my being mentally sharp. We were both in terrible shape with no sign of getting better. Neither of us could hold on to what we used to depend on. Could that be by design?

Along with everything else, I had been worrying about how we would make a living. *What would we do if both of us fell apart and were unable to function in the only way we knew how to succeed professionally?* After retiring from baseball, Dave began doing speaking appearances to earn a living. I wanted to help him, but so far I seemed to be more of a burden than a help. Was I supposed to let go of everything and trust God would take care of us? In my heart, I knew the answer was yes. Since I couldn't manage to hold on anyway, mentally I agreed to let go and let God.

In the next few weeks, I regained some strength and was able to be up and about more, so Donna and Frank moved out. Getting out of bed and forcing myself to participate in some family activities helped, but I had days when everything seemed so dark that I was overcome with the pain of my own despair. One day in June, I called Dr. McGowen and cried, "It's so hard! I can't take any more."

He said, "I know you need help, Jan, but I can't help you unless you'll receive it. You need counseling, or you need medication. Please—"

I panicked. "No! No!" I shouted into the receiver and hung up the phone. I was crying out for help, but when he offered it, I pulled back and refused the help I desperately needed.

In July, we went to Chicago because Dave was given the Danny Thompson Award. It's the Christian tribute to the baseball world awarded by Baseball Chapel. Until this time, I had not met anyone who had gone through anything like what I was going through. And even if people had gone through it, they didn't tell me. There we saw a friend who was associated with Baseball Chapel and had always appeared to me as an enthusiastic, happy-go-lucky Christian. He was one of the last people I would have expected to understand what I was experiencing, but he could see that something was wrong with me.

He came up to me and asked, "What's wrong? Are you suffering from depression?"

I said, "I think so."

"I've been there," he said. "You can get to the other side." Then he gave me some advice. He told me to start doing things that would put pluses in my column rather than minuses. He talked about the importance of good nutrition and taking vitamins. He also mentioned that he was on medication, but I played that down because I did not want to be on medication for depression. I still saw taking medication as some sort of defeat. Even though I didn't agree with all he said, I felt immensely relieved to know that a Christian I knew had been depressed as badly as I was and had come through it.

That night, we went to the All-Star game. I made it through three innings, then Dave had to take me home because I couldn't handle the noise. Again, I felt guilty for ruining this special occasion for Dave. I feared he might tire of me altogether, but he loved me and took care of me without complaining.

On July 17, 1990, Dave and I were scheduled to tape a segment to be aired on the Billy Graham Evangelistic Crusade. This was a great honor, and I wanted to share our hope in Jesus Christ, even though my hope was feeble because of my own weakness. We decided to share a Scripture that had almost become our motto. On a beautiful summer day, the crew taped Dave and me sitting together on a park bench, looking into each other's eyes, and reciting these words:

> Therefore we do not lose heart, though outwardly we are wasting away, yet inwardly we are being renewed day by day. For our light and momentary troubles are achieving for us an eternal glory that far outweighs them all. So we

fix our eyes not on what is seen, but on what is unseen. For what is seen is temporary, but what is unseen is eternal. (2 Corinthians 4:16–17)

Even though I firmly believed this Scripture to be true and I was trying to fix my eyes on what is unseen, I was still sinking deeper and deeper into depression. The more I became depressed, the greater the weight of guilt I carried. Dave's frustration was growing too. As an athlete, he had learned to just "suck it up" if he was in pain, and he couldn't understand why I was languishing. He was also frustrated and angry that I wasn't there for him to support him, and he was upset that he couldn't fix me. He took my depression as a personal failure, and he didn't like to fail, especially when it came to something as important as taking care of his wife.

I still had a hard time breathing, so I would put my hand to my chest whenever I had difficulty breathing. I don't know why; it was just my little quirk, and Dave would imitate me. He even got our friends who were around to imitate me; they would laugh whenever I made that gesture. They were probably trying to make me laugh, but to me it felt like mockery, and it hurt.

To me, my condition was no laughing matter. I kept thinking about what our friend had said about medication helping him get out of depression. But I knew our pastor was vehemently opposed to Christians' relying on medication. So I decided to go to our pastor for help. Our church had only about 150 members, few enough that I didn't feel I would be overburdening him by sharing my pain. We had a church picnic scheduled that weekend at a local lake; I would talk to him then.

The whole time we were at the picnic, I looked for an opportunity to talk to the pastor privately. When the opportunity came, I gathered up enough courage and greeted him.

"Pastor, please, I need you to pray for me." I could feel the tightness in my chest and thickness in my throat as I spoke, "I . . .

I'm not doing well. I mean, I think I'm depressed, and it keeps getting worse even though I'm seeking the Lord. I don't want to have to go on medication ..."

"Well, that's good to hear," he said.

"But I'm not well. I can feel myself sinking back down again. I need help. I need the elders to pray for me, to pray against this depression."

There, I had said it. It was hard to humble myself to admit my weakness and ask for help, but I did it.

He looked at me and shook his head ever so slightly. "Jan, if I called the elders together to pray for every woman who had an emotional problem, we wouldn't get anything else done. You just need to take this to the Lord. Just take it to the foot of the cross and leave it there."

I thought about the women of the church. Indeed, many of them had dealt with depression, and they were still suffering to varying degrees. None of them ever went to counseling because the pastor shamed anyone who did; but none of them seemed victorious over their depression either.

I was stunned, absolutely stunned at the pastor's lack of response. I was too stunned to get angry right then, but once the shock wore off, I knew that church was not the one for me. Even though it was a place where we had some close relationships and where our children attended school, I knew then that I wanted to find another church.

Dave hates to quit; he'd rather make every effort to work through the problems to make a positive change before he walks away. So he convinced me to stay for a while. However, since I had tried to get help from the pastor and found none available, I became open to other sources of help.

During that first week of August 1990, I was feeling so dark one day that I called Dr. McGowen again, even though I had hung up on him the last time. He was so concerned that he said, "Jan, you and Dave come to my office."

Dr. McGowen didn't suggest counseling again, but he said, "Jan, you and Dave are fighting two battles at this time; one is physical and one is spiritual. You are clinically depressed. I can help you with the physical battle so that you will be strong enough to fight the spiritual. I want to put you on Prozac. It's an antidepressant that should help you considerably. You have to do something to get back on track."

We were so weary and uncertain, we didn't argue. I finally accepted the fact (even though I'd fought it long and hard) that I needed medication. The doctors had told me so for a long time, and finally my life had grown so dark that I knew I was in trouble and needed help. So Dr. McGowen put me on Prozac and reassured me that I would start feeling better in two weeks.

That was in 1990 when Prozac was getting a lot of bad press, and everyone who found out I was on Prozac felt it was their obligation to tell me a new horror story about someone going berserk from using Prozac. Some guy on Prozac killed twelve people; another guy on Prozac killed his family and himself. The news media presented all these specials on the dangerous side-effects of Prozac, causing me to shiver in my boots. When I told Dave's mother about the Prozac, she told me, "That's the one they say is causing people to murder and commit suicide!"

All these rumors got to me, and I was terrified that I might lose my mind and hurt myself or my children. So I telephoned Dr. McGowen.

He said, "Jan, those rumors are false. I would put my wife on Prozac if she were in your condition. You need to be on antidepressants. Trust me! This publicity about Prozac is not true. This is a miracle drug that will help you!"

Even though I felt guilt and confusion about taking the medication, it worked extremely well for me. Within about two weeks I was able to drive a car, which I hadn't been able to do since my collapse at CBA four months earlier. I could drive only short distances, and I had to talk on the car phone so I wouldn't feel alone, but at least I wasn't agoraphobic anymore. My black mood persisted, but I was making progress. Within about three weeks my normal sleep pattern returned, and for the first time in many months I was able to sleep through the night.

On the few occasions that I heard about someone who had committed suicide, I went bonkers. It scared me. At the time, I was not suicidal, but I feared I was losing my mind and might do something dangerous.

At this time I read John 10:27–29 every day: "My sheep listen to my voice; I know them, and they follow me. I give them eternal life, and they shall never perish; no one can snatch them out of my hand. My Father, who has given them to me, is greater than all; no one can snatch them out of my Father's hand." The verses reassured me that no one—not me, nor Satan—could take me out of God's care.

It was a hot August day. Dave and the kids wanted to go swimming, and since I had been having some good days, they hoped I would join them. I could clearly see how much my children missed me. But this was a very dark day for me, and I did not have the energy to go with them. So Dave took the kids and headed over to the pool without me.

I was so angry at God. I paced the floor as my anger grew into rage. I went into my family room, and I shook my fist at God. I spoke out loud, "You know what . . . I can't feel you, I can't see you, I can't sense you, I don't even know if you exist anymore. And if you *do* exist, why aren't you helping me? I can't even go to the stupid pool with my kids!"

Still fuming with anger, I said, "You know what I need to do? I need to run. I'll just go back to the world. Just like in the beginning when I didn't understand you back in Colombia. I need to get busy; I need to fill my life up with things. I have enough money now . . . I could fill myself up with material things. I ought to just turn my back on you!"

But I couldn't. I knew I couldn't. Even with all its pleasures and promising distractions, I knew that the world could only offer a temporary solution. God offered the only eternal answer.

When I was a little girl, only five or six years old, I would sometimes get so mad at my parents that I would threaten to run away. I packed up my little suitcase with clothes, a few toys, and my favorite stuffed animal. Then I grabbed the handle of my little suitcase, stomped past my mom, and headed for the front door.

Mom would stand at the door with a sad expression on her face and say, "Oh, Jan, I hope you will be okay. We will miss you."

But I would not be dissuaded. I marched down the front steps, down the long driveway, and to the sidewalk. Then I stood there. Mom waved good-bye and closed the door. I looked out at the whole wide world. I could go anywhere I wanted, but suddenly I realized that there was only one place in the whole wide world where I would be safe and loved—back home. That realization carried me back up the driveway, through the front door, and into my mother's waiting arms.

This is what happened to me that day. When I finally decided to turn my back and run away from God, he let me walk to the edge. He let me walk to a place where I realized that no one loved me as he did. Just as my mother would not have let me really run away, God wouldn't either. I am his child; but in his great wisdom, he let me realize that nowhere else in the whole wide world, nowhere in all creation, can I go from his presence. He wouldn't let me go.

What a wonderful and humbling realization!

I was in the same dilemma that faced Jesus' disciples when many people were leaving Jesus because of his difficult teachings.

"You do not want to leave too, do you?" Jesus asked his twelve disciples.

Peter answered, "Lord, to whom shall we go? You have the words of eternal life. We believe and know that you are the Holy One of God" (John 6:66–69).

That's how I felt. Where else was I to go? God had me between a rock and a hard place. As David wrote:

> You hem me in—behind and before;
> you have laid your hand upon me. . . .
> Where can I go from your Spirit?
> Where can I flee from your presence?
> If I go up to the heavens, you are there;
> if I make my bed in the depths, you are there.
> If I rise on the wings of the dawn,
> if I settle on the far side of the sea,
> even there your hand will guide me,
> your right hand will hold me fast. (Psalm 139:5, 7–10)

All this time I thought I was holding on to God, grasping with all my earthly might not to let go. And that is precisely why God told me to let go. He knew that when I finally loosened my grip, I would realize he was holding me fast.

God's Word and his promises began to sink in. I realized, *I really do believe this!* And for the first time in months, I felt a glimmering of hope.

Twelve

Just Pull Yourself Together!

*T*he late September sunshine warmed my face as Dave and I climbed a hill in the mountains of Montana. We were in Montana on a retreat with the staff of Focus on the Family. Dr. James Dobson wasn't there because of his recent heart attack, but his staff welcomed us into their warm community. They had been very supportive since we were interviewed on their radio program shortly after Dave's comeback.

During the five months since my collapse, my whole world had seemed to close in on me. Looking up now, at the wide blue expanse, I understood why Montana was called "Big Sky Country." The sky seemed so much larger than I had remembered it. How many other days like this had been lost to me while I was crying in the darkness? Literally and figuratively, I felt as though I was coming out into the sunshine for the first time in months.

When Focus on the Family invited us to this retreat, I didn't want to go, but Dave insisted it would do us a world of good. He was right. The staff was very interested in what we had been going through as a result of Dave's cancer. They could see by my appearance that I had suffered, too. I was much thinner since the last time they saw me. Ruthie, one of the staff, later said that I looked like a skeleton with skin.

One afternoon we were all sitting around the pool in lounge chairs while Dave and I told them about my depression. The staff members listened with compassion. One of the men tried to encourage us by saying that he believed God would one day use me to minister to others who know the pain of depression. At the time, I felt so overwhelmed with my own pain that I could not begin to think about helping someone else. What a switch that was! God had brought me a long way from being the woman who thought it was her job to take care of everyone else.

I used the beautiful terrain as a form of therapy. Hiking became a way to face some of my fears. I climbed a mountain, went horseback riding, and made a conscious effort to rejoin the human race.

One day, Dave and I climbed a rocky hill together. He held my hand and looked back at me. "Jan, it's nice to have you back again, babe," he told me, smiling.

I knew what he meant. When I had been so absorbed in my own pain, we seemed to lose each other. We never stopped loving each other as a matter of choice, but at some point in our torturous journey, we disconnected. Now, for the first time in a long time, we were able to look into each other's eyes and share a sense of the love we had for each other.

"Dave, I'm so sorry that I let you down when you needed me," I said as we sat down on a grassy place to rest and talk.

He took my hand again. "I'm not concerned so much about your being there for me. I just want to make sure you are okay. I don't understand what happened to you. I'm just glad you're getting over it; it scared me. I'd just look at you, and I couldn't reach you. I didn't know what to say or do to snap you out of whatever it was you were going through. I missed you, Jan, I missed the old you."

I smiled sadly. "I almost forget what the old me was like," I replied. "There are times when I remember all I used to be able to do, and it seems like that was someone else. I don't know if you will ever have the old me back again, Dave. I'm trying. I'm trying every way I know."

"Look, babe," Dave said, "I don't want to put any pressure on you, but I know you have the strength. I'm praying you can find it again; but whatever happens, I'm going to love you. We're going to get through this together with the Lord's help."

Dave put both arms around me and kissed me. It wasn't like the kiss shared in victory on our ninth wedding anniversary at the high point of his career. It was a kiss sobered by the adversity of life, a kiss that held a promise of love, no matter what. I let myself revel in the sense of Dave's love, now that I was able to feel something other than my own pain. *Had he been loving me like this all along and I couldn't feel it?* I wondered. I wondered what else I had missed when I was consumed with my dark confusion and exhaustion.

He held me as we looked at the clouds moving carelessly across the big sky. "I think the medicine is helping me," I said. "I'm starting to feel alive again. Maybe soon I'll be strong enough to get off it. I don't want to become too dependent on it."

Dave had never been completely comfortable with my being on medication anyway. He still couldn't understand why I was depressed or why the Lord didn't help me get over it, but he allowed me to follow the doctor's recommendation because he was so concerned about my condition. We both felt tremendous pressure to get me off Prozac; our pastor continually made comments that showed his disapproval. Dave was on the board of elders, and because I had "given in to the world" (in the pastor's mind) by relying on medication, Dave was put in an awkward position with the other men loyal to our church.

When we got home from our weekend in Montana, Dave's health became the focus of attention. Dave was supposed to travel to California for some speaking appearances and book signings. In

Montana, he had complained of some flu-like symptoms, so when we got home, he went to Dr. McGowen, hoping to get some antibiotics before his trip. The doctor discovered that Dave had a staph infection throughout his whole body.

"You could have died," Dr. McGowen scolded him. "You have to get to the hospital immediately."

Dave protested, "I have to go to California."

"You're not going anywhere!" the doctor stated firmly. "You're sick, and you're going straight to the hospital!"

The groups in California had to settle for a videotape of Dave from his hospital bed, where he stayed for the next five days.

Through September and into October, I continued to feel better. I was able to drive, felt like going out more often, and saw myself making definite headway. My goal was not to find and maintain a healthy balance; it was to get well enough so I didn't need the medication. Once I was doing better, I assumed I didn't need counseling or medication. So at the end of October, I asked Dr. McGowen to wean me off the medication. I thought I would be strong enough then if I continued to rely on God, and since this decision agreed with what we were hearing continually from our pastor and close friends from church, my decision was met with approval all around.

If I had understood then what I now understand, I would have been able to predict my coming downfall. Unfortunately, I was still operating with a faulty understanding of my physical and related emotional condition. So when I began to slide slowly back into depression—waking early with feelings of foreboding, losing my ability to concentrate, experiencing panic attacks, and retreating to my bed—I panicked. "Dave, I'm going down again. I'm going down."

At this time Dave was still sick, the flesh on his arm being eaten away by staph infection that the antibiotics couldn't reach. He was fighting his own valiant battle; he couldn't help me, nor could he understand me. We didn't make the logical connection that my worsening condition was a natural result of coming off the medication without doing anything else to deal with the underlying issues. He was exasperated and thought it was time for me to stop feeling sorry for myself and put myself together.

"Janice, look at me," he said, pointing at his arm. "Look at what I'm going through. I don't know what to tell you. You've got to come to a point where you decide to get better. When I was playing ball, I learned to push beyond the pain to do the job I had to do. We need you, and you need to get better. So just push past the pain, get out of bed, and face life with me. We have the Lord. We can do this with God's help."

Dave's frustration bordered on anger, but I could see how hard he was trying to motivate me to get beyond the darkness.

We were wandering around in a spiritual wilderness, unsure of what was coming next. For me, each step was taken with a sense of futility. Dave had been reading a book about great men and women of God who had all gone though wilderness experiences. He was gaining hope that God was using this time of uncertainty and suffering as preparation for another stage in our journey. He tried to share the things he was learning that helped him. While I was glad Dave had a source of hope, his hope did not automatically transfer to me. I knew I needed help, and Dave's pep talks were not enough to pull me out of the depression.

That winter, Dave's arm continued to worsen. Every day I had to change his bandages and clean his wound. He started with one hole in his arm and ended up with three. His arm was dying, the flesh was wasting away, and he was gradually losing mobility and the use of his arm.

I felt like I was in a free fall. I couldn't get help from my church, I wanted to avoid going back on medication, and Dave was adamant that I not go back to the psychiatrist or the counselor. He urged me to face whatever this was and find some way to pull myself together. I was determined to try, but I wished Dave could understand what was happening to me. I tried to explain.

"Dave, it feels like I'm in a fog. Everything is foggy inside my mind. I feel drunk, like my perceptions are all distorted. If I knew I was drunk or under the influence of something identifiable, I could withstand the feeling. But I feel like this when I haven't been drinking or taking anything, and I can't snap out of it. It's a scary feeling. It's real, and I can't just make it go away. I've tried. I try every day."

"Jan, stop trying to analyze everything," he said impatiently. "You're so introspective. Just give yourself a break and try to stop thinking about how you're feeling." Dr. McGowen had also encouraged me not to focus obsessively on my feelings, because the more I checked my emotional temperature, the more disturbed I became. Dave reminded me, "The doctor said to quit thinking about it, so just quit."

I was going down again, whether Dave understood or not, but I wasn't out for the count. I started looking for books at the Christian bookstore that might help me find a ray of hope and understanding. I picked up *When Your World Makes No Sense* (now called *Changes That Heal*) by Dr. Henry Cloud. The book confirmed what I already knew: I was depressed; I needed help; I had a husband who couldn't help because he didn't understand; and I would definitely not find help from a church that was covering up its ignorance and lack of power with religious catchphrases.

In March of 1991, we were still attending that church because I was waiting for Dave to make the move to another church. One Sunday, Dave was out of town, so I went alone. Usually I didn't pay much attention to the sermon since the pastor was unable or unwilling to help me, but that day the preaching was obviously and pointedly referring to me.

"If you are depressed," the pastor asserted, "you don't need medication, you don't need counseling, you don't need to go running after everything the world has to offer. That will only open you up to the power of Satan and take you further and further into the realm of the Enemy. By turning away from the Word of God as your only source of truth, you invite, no, you welcome, the attack of the Enemy. No wonder you are depressed! You need to repent and sacrifice yourself at the base of the cross!"

At the close of the service, I got up and walked out, determined not to return. I'd done enough reading to know that what he was saying about me was not biblical. When I told Dave about the pastor's sermon, he agreed it was time to find a new church. We never went back.

Our closest friends from church were living with us at the time while preparing to move to another house. When we left the church, they remained, so we heard the reaction of the pastor and the congregation. The pastor taught them that I was going down again because we had left the spiritual covering of the church and, therefore, our family was susceptible to demonic attack. Sadly, many of our friends agreed with him.

Even though I knew we were doing the right thing, leaving was painful. I lost my friends and the community that had taken care of us when we were most vulnerable. But I was somehow aware that God was back in control.

I decided to visit a charismatic church where I had heard that the people were filled with joy. I wanted to feel the joy. I knew God said we would face adversity, but I also knew there was to be a source of joy even in the face of adversity. This charismatic church had a lot of joy! I went to the front, near the altar, and I cried about my depression. Someone asked what I needed prayer for, and I told them. The people gathered around me, laid hands on me to pray, and anointed me with oil. They prayed that I would be freed from my depression.

God honored that prayer because it was a major turning point for me. God was leading me, and I didn't even know it. As I was walking back to my seat, a woman stopped me and said that she had a word from God for me. It was Psalm 25:3–5. It says, "No one whose hope is in you will ever be put to shame, but they will be put to shame who are treacherous without excuse." She knew nothing about me, but she was describing my situation. I had been under the influence of a pastor who was shaming me from the pulpit and a church community that was shaming me because I left.

The psalm continues, "Show me your ways, O LORD, teach me your paths; guide me in your truth and teach me, for you are God my Savior, and my hope is in you all day long." This verse was precisely what I needed at that moment.

I didn't go back to that charismatic church because Dave didn't feel comfortable there, but the Lord used that church and that woman to encourage me. I will always be grateful to God for the way he used their ministry in my life when I needed it.

We wanted to be confident that we would get sound biblical teaching, so we chose a church where the pastor had solid theological training. I discovered that the pastor's wife, Lori, had worked at a Minirth-Meier Clinic while her husband was in seminary. The associate pastor's wife, Beth, told me her husband had spent two months at the Minirth-Meier Clinic in treatment for depression. There was no shame here. I had just left a church that condemned all forms of counseling, Christian or secular. Now, God had led us to a church where they ministered from a position of acceptance.

My emotional pain was apparent to these caring people from the outset. Lori called me; Beth also called me. They wanted to find out what was troubling me and how they might help. Lori said, "Jan, you can get well. There is treatment that will help you if you are willing to seek it. Will Dave agree to let you go into the hospital for treatment? We'll make arrangements and help you in any way that we can."

"Well, okay, I guess . . ." On the phone I sounded unsure, but inside, hope began to build. It sounded so great! Help might be just one phone call away. Now all I had to do was figure out how to present the idea to Dave in such a way that he would agree to let me go to the hospital.

That afternoon, when Dave came home, we sat at the kitchen table, and I approached the subject of hospitalization very carefully because I knew I was walking on a tightrope with him. It was May 1991, and Dave still had the staph infection, three holes in his arm that drained constantly, and a hole in his stomach (an ulcer from all of the medication that he was taking, which was undiagnosed at the time). He was worn-out.

I knew the thought of my going into the hospital might send him over the edge for a number of reasons, so I proceeded with caution.

I said, "David, I talked with Beth this morning, the associate pastor's wife, about what her husband went through. He went through a really bad depression."

"Oh, really." His facial expression was not encouraging.

"Yeah, and they admitted him to Minirth-Meier Clinic. Dave, he was as depressed as I am. This program helped him get over the depression. Look at him now; you'd never know he was ever depressed."

Dave sighed. "We've been over this time and time again!"

"David, please . . . would you just consider letting me go to Minirth-Meier to get some counseling?"

"You've had counseling. It just made you worse. It upset you more. It just stirred things up."

"But this is different! Lori and Beth think I should go inpatient. If I went into the hospital, you wouldn't have to put up with all this—"

"No!"

"David, please, let me go as an inpatient. I want to be free from this depression!" I could see his anger building, but I was willing to risk it. I was fighting for my freedom now. "They have everything set up. . . ."

"They what? Who has everything set up? Where was I when they were setting everything up?" Dave demanded.

"Beth and Lori. They have everything set up. All we have to do is call. I didn't call; I wouldn't call without your approval. David, maybe we could go together . . ."

He was so angry at me that he picked up the phone and threw it as hard as he could. He smashed it to smithereens and shouted, "Here, call our counselor! There, there's your phone, call . . . make your blankety-blank phone call!" And he stormed out.

Sobbing, I bent down to pick up the pieces of the phone. The shattered phone was a fitting symbol of my situation. After spending my whole life convincing people that I didn't need help, I was finally calling out for help, trying to communicate my desperate need. But my cries for help had fallen on deaf ears, and one of my primary means of communication lay shattered at my feet. I couldn't get through to anyone.

I had come a long way. I no longer tried to control my own life, nor was I completely losing my grip and cursing God. But after Dave's blowup, I felt as though I was falling again. I didn't feel that I could go against my husband's wishes, so I cried out to God, my last refuge. *Oh, Lord, do you hear me? Will you hear my prayer and rescue me?*

God was at work in his own way, for his own purposes, to accomplish his will in my life. His will was good, as I trusted it would be, but the way that he had charted for me was not on my map. He was determined to surprise me, whether I liked it or not.

Thirteen

Falling into the Strong Hands of God

A week after Dave broke the phone, on May 19, we were scheduled to go to California. Dave made a commitment for us to do an interview with Dr. James Dobson for the Focus on the Family radio program. I truly did not want to go. The depression seemed to be deepening. The thought of packing a suitcase seemed overwhelming enough, and the thought of flying on an airplane was even worse. I just wanted to stay home where I felt safe, but Dave pleaded with me, "Jan, I don't want to go on this trip alone. Please come with me."

I felt so frustrated as I tried to explain, "I can't pack another suitcase—it's too hard! And I can't bear the thought of getting on a plane."

"What?" His voice rose with each word. "What do you mean? Something as simple as packing a suitcase and flying on a jet? You've done it a thousand times before."

"I know it sounds silly," I replied, "but please try to understand. I can't bear the thought of doing anything right now."

Dave persisted. "Look, I will accept that this is difficult for you. But I will help you pack, and I'll be with you on the plane. I'll hold your hand the whole way if you want, but you must come with me. Besides, Dr. Dobson is counting on us doing the interview together."

After much hesitation, I agreed. I took comfort in knowing Dave was beginning to accept that I needed help. Knowing he would be sensitive to my condition and be beside me all the way encouraged me to go with him. Looking back, it scares me to think how strongly I resisted going on what would be the most pivotal weekend of my life.

While waiting at the airport, I read a little booklet someone gave me: *The Tyranny of the Urgent* by Charles Hummel. This booklet helped me see how to approach a new way of living. It helped me understand how my tendency to respond to the urgent demands all around me and my lack of rest contributed to my downfall. What light it brought me!

The booklet told how Jesus took time to go away by himself to be with his Father. After his disciples had been out ministering, he pulled them away for a time of rest. This really grabbed my attention because I was saying yes to my kids, and yes to my husband, and yes to friends, but I rarely said yes to myself. My set of rules dictated that if a need existed, I needed to fill it; but physically, I couldn't do it all. I felt relieved that even Jesus, God in the flesh, needed to take time for his own restoration.

I had always believed that any need that came my way was of God—and there was so much need around me, and not enough of me to satisfy it. The booklet addressed how, at the end of his life, Jesus could say, "It is finished!" even though many of the needs of those around him were left untended. Jesus' life "showed a wonderful balance, a sense of timing" because "he prayerfully waited for his Father's instructions and for the strength to follow them. Jesus had no divinely drawn blueprint; he discerned the Father's will day by day in a life of prayer. By this means, he warded off the urgent and accomplished the important."[1]

Well, I no longer had the strength to respond to the urgent needs all around me. I had come to the point where all I could do was to pray, seek the Father's will, and follow wherever he might lead me on this journey. That is why I felt so encouraged as I read this booklet at the airport. I realized that maybe I was doing all that was necessary—even in my depressed condition.

Dave was still a problem. I didn't know how I was going to deal with him. I knew him well enough to know that confrontation would only aggravate our difference of opinion, and I was too wiped out to manipulate him into letting me get the kind of help I needed. But I still had in my mind, somehow, some way, I was going to get myself help.

Going into the radio show, I was depressed. Mornings were always much worse than the evenings. I don't know why, but I would be so depressed when I woke up. If I worked at it and got myself going, I would feel better as the day went on.

We had promised Dr. Dobson we would give his audience an update on how we were doing. Of course, we were falling apart. Knowing that Dr. Dobson was a psychologist, I secretly harbored the desire in my heart that God might use him to help me.

When we recorded the radio program, I didn't even try to keep up the good image anymore. By this time, that was over. I was ready to be real! We talked openly about our wilderness walk, how we didn't know what would happen with Dave's arm, which was totally useless to Dave by now. We openly told them that we saw no light. We just said it right out, "We don't know what's gonna happen. We're weary. We're tired. We're worn-out!"

At one point, Dr. Dobson asked me how I was doing with my depression. "Well . . ." I hesitated. "Some days are better than others, but I'm hurting. I'm certainly not over it yet." Dave talked more optimistically because he was starting to make sense of his wilderness walk, but I couldn't.

After the interview, Dr. Dobson ushered us into his office. "How are you doing?" he asked, looking me directly in the eyes.

I started to tell him what I had been going through. As I spoke freely, he sat there and listened with tears in his eyes.

Finally, he said gently, "Jan, I know what you're going through. My father went through a similar instance when he was thirty-eight. He thought he would never be able to preach again. But you know what the problem was, Jan? He was exhausted!"

Then he said to Dave, "Look at her, Dave. She's exhausted. She's exhausted emotionally and physically."

Dave told him, "Well, I don't know what to do for her. You know, she's been reading this Minirth-Meier stuff. I don't know what to think. I've read some things by an author I respect, and he does a fine job of slamming the Christian counseling movement. I don't know whom I can trust. What do you think?"

James Dobson looked at him and said, "Dave, I know Paul Meier. That man spends time in the Word and prayer every day before he writes or treats patients. He's a very godly man!"

Dave was surprised. "Really?"

"Yes, he's a very godly man." Dr. Dobson assured him. "Get Jan help, Dave. She needs it, and there's nothing wrong with it!"

Right there in Dr. Dobson's office, I could see Dave's mind starting to change. I was thrilled! What a privilege! I mean, what more could a woman ask than to have Dr. James Dobson tell her husband to do the very thing she wanted him to do?

God wasn't finished yet. As we were leaving Dr. Dobson's office, our literary agent, Sealy Yates, turned to me and told me he had a book for me to read. He said he knew what I had been going through and thought this book might help. I can't tell you how shocked I was when I found out the book was *When Your World Makes No Sense.*

I said, "I can't believe this. This is the book I've been reading, and it's been a great help! How did you know about it?"

He said, "Well Jan, John Townsend and Henry Cloud are my new clients."

"Really?" I gasped.

"Yes!" He grinned.

"Sealy, do you think you could make an appointment with Henry Cloud and let me meet with him?" At this point, I felt strong enough to override any objection that Dave might have. Also, I knew I had Dr. Dobson to back me up. This was my chance, and I wasn't about to miss it. Besides, I could sense Dave's heart softening. Even though he is a man of great strength and conviction, he does listen to God's voice when he senses the Holy Spirit's leading.

Sealy tried to get us an appointment with Dr. Henry Cloud. He wasn't available, but Sealy was able to get an appointment with his partner, John Townsend, for Sunday afternoon. I was so excited; God was taking care of me. I knew it, and I think Dave sensed it, too.

We met Dr. John Townsend on Sunday afternoon in his southern California office. He came into his office wearing his Dockers, and sat down, swinging his leg over the side of his chair and tucking his other leg up underneath him. He wasn't anything like our preconceived idea of what a counselor might look like. Casual and confident, he looked like one of us. We both liked him immediately.

After listening to my story, he looked at me and said, "Jan, you know what? You're off the scale. Do you know how many stress points you have? I'm surprised that you're even here today! You're off the charts with loss and pain and stress. It's amazing that you two are still married with all the struggles you have."

This guy pulled no punches. But what he said made sense, and we listened.

"Neither of you have boundaries in your life," he continued. "In my opinion, Satan tried to take advantage of that, coming in as an Angel of Light to try to destroy both of you! I'm glad you're out of that church."

Then he looked Dave square in the eye and said, "Dave, your wife is sick. She is physically and emotionally sick. When she tells you she is at point A, and she knows she needs to get to point B and she can't get there, believe her! She can't get there; she doesn't know the way. She needs the help of someone else to teach her how to get there. She needs treatment, and that's the purpose of a counselor in her life, to help teach her the right, healthy way to live. And Dave, I hate to tell you this, but you're depressed, too. You're burned out, and you need help. You're not the one who can help her; it has to be someone outside. Do you feel threatened, Dave, because you can't take care of your own wife?"

Dave said, "Yeah, I do!"

Dr. Townsend said, "Well, let me remove that burden from your shoulders because you're not the one to help her. She needs professional help!"

At that point, I brought up the issue of allowing me to go for inpatient treatment. I had packed my bags for California with enough clothes for three weeks, thinking I might stay for inpatient treatment at Minirth Meier Clinics West. I did not want to go home without having received help.

But Dr. Townsend said, "You might need to go inpatient eventually, but that's not the first resort by a long shot. You've tried nothing, as far as I'm concerned. You've not tried the proper medication. When you go on medication, you need to have counseling, too." And he said, "My advice would be for you to see a psychiatrist about going back on medication. Get some good Christian counseling, but try to stick with it this time. If I can't find you a counselor I can personally recommend in your area and if your condition worsens, then we'll look into getting you into a clinic."

God didn't go halfway when he went to work on my behalf. He gave me one of the best counselors! Anybody else might have rubbed Dave the wrong way; but everything about Dr. Townsend was just what Dave needed to win him over. God took Dave's feelings into account and arranged for me to get help in a way with which he felt comfortable.

John Townsend recommended Dr. Loren Sommers in Ohio. I started seeing him twice a week, for two hours each time, and Dave came with me. It was an hour and fifteen minutes away, but it gave Dave and me two-and-a-half hours during the drive to talk, plus two hours with the counselor. Dave originally went just to satisfy me because I was the one who was sick (or so he thought). But six weeks after we started counseling, he was the one on the couch!

All this happened without my arranging anything. God did it all. Even when I couldn't feel him, even when I couldn't sense him, even when I wasn't holding on to him anymore, God worked on my behalf. He didn't need me to do a thing!

I thought back to Dave's comeback and saw the similarities. That was not something we orchestrated either. In fact, we didn't know Dave was going to make it back until he was on the mound. If anything, I worked against Dave's comeback in an unspoken effort to protect us from disappointment. My pessimism was just another way of trying to protect myself and control my life, but it didn't work. When I faced far worse than my worst imaginings, something unexpected and wonderful happened. I realized that God is in control and God is good—even when bad things happen in our lives.

Even though I didn't know what I might have to go through next, I could rest and accept it. Because now I knew that when I let go, I would fall into the strong hands of God.

Fourteen

Rotting Flesh

*E*ven though Dave and I were relieved to be facing life from a unified position once more, we still faced daily challenges. Dave's arm was a mess, and I had to tend it. Daily I cleaned out the holes, dipped gauze in antibiotics, then packed the swabs into the open wounds.

Since previous radiation therapy had destroyed the capillaries that would have delivered the antibiotics, our last resort to fight the infection and try to save his arm was to apply antibiotics directly on the sores. The staph infection found little pockets of flesh where it could hide and continue eating away at the arm that had once been the pride of the San Francisco Giants.

When we started counseling with Dr. Sommers in May 1991, God began showing me areas in my life that were like Dave's arm. Parts of my inner nature were rotting, and they needed attention as much as Dave's arm did.

I had been studying a teaching tape by Dr. Charles Stanley called *Seven Stages of Spiritual Growth*.[1] The tape outlined seven steps common to those who seek to follow the Lord.

The first step is *unbelief*, our state before we come to believe in Jesus as our Savior. Second comes *salvation*, when we trust Christ to save us from our sins by his finished work on the cross. The third step is *service*, when we feel that God has done so much for us that we ought to repay him with good deeds. Fourth is *frustrated inadequacy*, when we do our best to serve God and realize that we are inadequate.

The fifth step occurs when we ask God to fill us so we can work by the power of the Holy Spirit. It is the step of *spiritual dependency*. Sixth is the *battle of preprogrammed bondage*, when we must battle the programming we received as we were growing up that keep us in bondage. And finally, seventh, is the *exchanged life*, when we stop living in the flesh, serving from our own strength. Instead, we begin to allow Christ to live through us.

God seemed to be leading me to the point of the exchanged life. I had come from unbelief to faith in Christ, and I immediately had felt the need to give something back to God by serving him in my own strength. I kept trying and serving until I realized I wasn't able to do it all—the stage of frustrated inadequacy. But I kept pushing myself anyway, until I collapsed. Then came the valley of depression and a path that led me to utter dependence on the Holy Spirit.

So far my journey had taken me through stages one through five, just as Dr. Charles Stanley had described them. And now I was stuck in stage six, battling with my preprogrammed bondage to self-sufficiency.

Was I ready for God to open me up and identify the areas of my life that held me captive? Dr. Stanley said that many Christians turn back at stage six because the prospect of having God go deeply into one's life can be quite frightening. But I sensed that God had sent me this tape at the appropriate time. I didn't want to go back to a life of frustrated inadequacy. Instead, I resolved to face the truth about myself, no matter how ugly it turned out to be.

With the help of my counselor, I began to delve into my past, to examine the programming that had shaped me. And for the first time, I realized some negative results of my upbringing.

Mom had painted an unrealistic picture of life to me. She had taught me that I could do anything I put my mind to—anything! But that was not the whole truth. She failed to teach me that I could do all things only through Christ who strengthened me. Living my entire life on the basis of this well-intentioned lie created a faith in my own self-sufficiency that proved to be my downfall.

I thought I was being a good Christian by depending on my own strength to do God's work. I became the savior for everyone in need around me, instead of relying on the Savior. My primary weakness of the flesh was dependence on myself alone. I would manipulate relationships, even by helping others, in a way that stroked my ego. A lot of times, I was a caretaker so that people would need me. Taking care of people fulfilled a selfish need in me, while making me appear to be a generous and good Christian.

I put my children on the back burner because motherhood made me feel inadequate. I have children who are just like me—strong-willed. Sometimes I could force them to act the way I wanted, but I couldn't change their insides. And that frustrated me.

So I did numerous good deeds in the community, in the name of Christianity, trying to feel good about myself. I headed up a cookbook drive where all the donations went to the Children's Hospital in San Diego. I felt good about myself: I was a doer, an organizer, an achiever. Everybody would pat me on the back and say, "Oh, you're so wonderful. Oh, you've done all of this." But they didn't know I was avoiding one of my primary responsibilities: being a mother.

When I was a child, my mother was always there physically, but she never played with me. When she would agree to play a game with me, it would be such a thrill. Now I was like her. I had to force myself to sit down and play a game with my kids. Playing with my kids didn't feed my ego. Organizing the latest fund drive did.

It blew me away when I learned that trying to meet every need that came to my attention was a selfish act. It was selfish because my activity was an attempt to soothe over every problem around me that made me uncomfortable and to do things that would make me look good in the eyes of others. It was hypocrisy.

My busy life of doing good wasn't corrected by the church; it was applauded. Our church misused the Scripture, "Do not forsake the gathering of yourselves together," by implying that every time the church doors open, you should be in church. Whoever was not there was looked upon as not spiritual enough.

I was working myself to death trying to please God, save people, and become a better person. I was doing all the right things for all the wrong reasons.

These realizations felt like God was doing exploratory surgery in my soul. It was painful. And I didn't like what he uncovered. Like Dave, I was living with a rotting piece of flesh.

Would I be willing to let it go?

Fifteen

Giving Consent

One day in early June, a friend drove me to see the counselor because Dave was in New York having his arm examined. On the way, I received a call on the car phone.

"Jan," Dave said, calling from the hospital, "the doctors agree that it's time."

"Time for what—to amputate?"

Since last summer, we had known the time might come when it would be necessary to amputate. We didn't talk about it; it was one of those silent understandings that a married couple often shares.

"Well, they have to do another surgery right away. There is an outside chance they may be able to save the arm . . ." (I noticed he called it "the arm," already distancing himself from that part of him that had once been his greatest asset.) " . . . but before I go under this time I have to sign a consent form, agreeing to whatever degree of amputation is necessary."

I was quiet for a moment.

"Jan, are you all right?"

"Yeah, I'm on the way to the counselor's office. Look at how the Lord prepared us for this. I'm sure I'll be all right. Dave, are you all right?"

He sounded very serene. "Yeah, babe; I think it may be time."

Dave was ready to be relieved of the rotting flesh he'd been carrying around for too long. If someone had come to him while he was still pitching and told him he was going to have to lose his pitching arm, he probably would have rather died. But Dave's arm was no longer an asset. It had stopped being useful months ago and became a burden, a painful appendage that he had to lift with his other hand just to rest it on the table. His arm no longer made him feel like a star; now it only kept him from playing freely with his kids for fear they might bump it and break it again. It kept us from snuggling close together. It was like extra baggage that carried with it the threat of death. I shared Dave's acceptance of something that would have been unthinkable a few years before.

The surgery was scheduled immediately for June 18, 1991. Dave signed the consent forms the night before the surgery. He signed it with his right (nondominant) hand; his surrender was complete. The rest was up to the discretion of the surgeons. As they wheeled Dave into surgery, he lifted his left arm with his right hand, waving his left hand at the small group of us: Dave's parents, a few close friends, and me. He acted as if his arm were a toy.

"Say bye-bye to Mr. Arm," Dave joked.

I looked at my strong, brave husband as he yielded so graciously to whatever God had for him, and I had to smile. We still had hopes that they might be able to save his arm, but at that point, I, too, had surrendered to whatever God and the surgeons deemed best. When they came back out to tell us that the amputation was necessary, I was able to bear it.

Dave had put all his confidence in God and his surgeons—even though he knew he might lose his arm. He simply let go and trusted himself to God as they wheeled him toward that operating room. I was deeply impressed by his surrender because I was struggling with a personal issue of surrender in my life.

I had been reading a book called *Let Go* by Fenelon, a man who lived in seventeenth-century France. One of the letters he wrote to encourage persecuted Christians in his time spoke directly to me. As I sat waiting for the surgeons to amputate Dave's arm, this is what I read:

> I am told, my dear child in the Lord, that you are suffering from sickness. I want you to know that I suffer along with you, for I love you dearly; but I cannot but adore our wonderful Lord who permits you to be tried in this way. And I pray that you will adore Him along with me. You must never forget those days when you were so lively and energetic and as there's no doubt, this was hard on your health. And I rather think that the suffering you are going through now is the natural consequence of your high-pressured living.
>
> In this time of physical weakness, I pray that you become more and more aware of your spiritual weakness. I don't want you to remain weak, for while the Lord ministers to you and gives strength to your body, I pray that He will also minister strength to your soul and that weakness will finally be conquered. But you need to understand that you cannot become strong until first you are aware of your weakness. It is amazing how strong we can become, when we begin to realize what weaklings we are. It is in weakness that we can admit our mistakes and correct ourselves by confessing them. It is in weakness that our minds are open to enlightenment from others. It is in weakness that we are authoritative in nothing and say the most clear-cut things with simplicity and consideration for others. In weakness, we do not object to being criticized and we easily submit to censor. At the same time we criticize no one without absolute necessity. We give advice only to those who desire it and even then we speak with love and without being dogmatic. We speak from a desire to help, rather than a desire to create a reputation for wisdom.

So much of my self-sufficiency was associated with my strength of mind, my intellect, and what I knew. Even when I helped others, it wasn't from the pure motive of just wanting to help; that was mixed with a desire to create a reputation. Fenelon had me pegged! In that waiting room, I thought about how our trials had taken us progressively in the direction of weakness. I wondered, *Could God be using these experiences to get us to rely on him instead of relying on our own strength?*

I wasn't sure, but I told God, "Okay, Lord, I admit it; some things in my life so easily get out of control; I know there are patterns that aren't healthy in me, and I don't have the power to control what drives me. I give up; I need you to take over."

After long hours of waiting, Dr. Brennan finally informed us that the amputation was over. He told Dave's parents and me that we could go to the recovery room to see Dave. It's good that the grace of God was covering me, because I was not prepared for what I saw: Not only was his arm gone, but his shoulder was gone also. It looked like half of his body was missing.

Dave smiled drowsily as we walked up beside his bed. I smiled back to cover my shock and kissed Dave reassuringly, holding back my tears until after I left the recovery room. Dave's mom and dad also kept up a good front for his sake. But when we left the room, we cried together.

My tears flowed from a mixture of relief and sorrow. I cried from relief that our battle was over. I knew that the radical amputation was necessary to make sure the margin was wide enough that the tumor would not return, and I was grateful that the surgeon had played it safe.

Yet I also cried at the loss of a large portion of my husband's body. Remembering how healthy and handsome Dave's body had been, I felt a deep sense of loss caused by the sight of what was left. It was hard to think of the adjustments he would have to make. Seeing him with his body irreparably changed, spoke to me of the changes that were sure to come. My tears said what I had no words sufficient to express. And yet, God's grace was covering us. I had a peace that was beyond understanding, a peace that assured me we would not have to face these changes alone.

When Dave recovered from his amputation, we were surprised by the new freedom he enjoyed. He could wrestle with the kids again, and we could touch and hold each other without worry. The feelings of loss came later, as we learned to grieve, but our initial reaction was relief that the uncertainty was over and the risk removed. At last, Dave was no longer living in bondage to his dead flesh.

In a spiritual sense, I needed surgery, too, just as much as Dave needed surgery. I needed to trust God just as Dave had showed complete trust in the surgeons when he signed his consent forms. I had to give spiritual consent for God to do whatever he deemed best with the areas of my nature that had become a burden to me.

Before Dave's surgery, his doctor made it clear to us that his arm would never get better. At one point the doctor took me aside and said, "Jan, it's better just to get it off him. It will be a relief to him because it's dead." Now it seemed God was saying the same thing to me about trusting in my own strength. It was as though he took me aside and said, "Jan, your reliance on yourself is like trying to revive the flesh. Your selfish, sinful nature is never going to get better; it's dead; it's rotting away, corrupt through and through. Your own strength and goodness will never be sufficient for the life I want you to live."

I knew this to be true. During the time we were watching Dave's arm waste away, I, too, saw the nature of my human frailty, and it was ugly.

The only remedy the Bible gave for my rotting flesh of sin was crucifixion. Galatians 2:20 says, "I have been crucified with Christ and I no longer live, but Christ lives in me." That was the option for which God was asking me to give my consent.

Jeremiah 17:5–7 spelled out my options just as clearly. "Cursed is the one who trusts in man [human nature], who depends on flesh for his strength and whose heart turns away from the LORD. . . . But blessed is the man [or woman] who trusts in the LORD, whose confidence is in him."

I agreed to give my consent for God to do whatever he wanted in my life. And just as Dave and I were surprised by the sense of relief we felt after his amputation, I was surprised by the release and peace I found by surrendering my life to God and not relying only on myself. I had a sense of knowing that God would walk me through this life. For me, this was a whole new way of looking at life, a perspective born of suffering and enduring many trials.

Dave's surgery was a one-time deal; the surgery God was doing on my sinful nature was ongoing. But we both came through our respective surgeries in the protective care of our heavenly Father.

As I look back now, I am amazed at the way God orchestrated events to prepare us for what he knew was coming. He arranged for us to get into counseling just in time. He brought me to a point of spiritual surrender at the same time Dave surrendered his arm to the surgeon's knife. The prognosis for both of us: life! God knew better than I where my journey was to take me. I was aiming for perfection; he brought me to a better place, a place of grace and peace.

Sixteen

Light Dawns Across the Valley

*A*fter Dave's amputation in June 1991, we weren't sure what direction his career would take. We were still trying to work out some way to stay connected to baseball, the only professional life Dave had ever known. He thought about a position with Baseball Chapel, but doors weren't opening there. Then he thought about working for Focus on the Family, so we looked into living near Colorado Springs, Colorado. But we proceeded carefully, waiting and praying, wanting to be sure we were following God's lead, not just striking out haphazardly.

From 1991 until 1993, Dave and I continued a long, slow process of recovery. In May 1991 we hired two women to answer the continual flow of correspondence. Dave was doing speaking appearances, so some of the mail included requests for speaking that required a timely response. In August we started the Dave Dravecky Foundation. In September we began writing our book *When You Can't Come Back*. And in October 1991 we were interviewed by Barbara Walters on *20/20*. All along, we continued in counseling and made small steps toward a healthier life.

In January 1993, we met with Sealy and Susan Yates to pray and set goals for our future. We both longed for a fresh start and gravitated toward a move to Colorado Springs. With Dave speaking all over the country, the central location would make travel less taxing. We also liked being near so many fine Christian ministries in that area. Whatever happened to Dave's career, we knew we could carry out any option from Colorado. Besides, the idea of living in the beautiful Rocky Mountains appealed to us. Maybe that reflected our desire to get out of the emotional valley we had been living in for so long.

We discussed the merits of such a move with counselors, ministry leaders, family, and trusted friends. I was still recovering from depression, but I was stable and able to function fairly well by this time. I had been off antidepressant medication for almost a year and had resumed my role in the family. We knew that any move would be stressful but were assured that I would be fine if I continued counseling. After five months of careful consideration, we made our decision and moved near Colorado Springs in the summer of 1993.

We now live at the base of the front range of the Rocky Mountains. The sky is big and beautiful and the cloud formations breathtaking. Many beautiful storms form over the Rockies and then come over us. The lightning can be spectacular, and our family watches it as if it were a fireworks show. My favorite scene is after the storm rolls over and the sun finds openings in the clouds to peek its way through. The shining rays of sunlight cut through the darkness, coloring the drab landscape of the valley below with various shades of light.

While this heavenly play of light coming through the dark clouds is a fairly common occurrence, it never escapes our notice. Many times Dave and I have been driving along the highway down the hill from where we live, and Tiffany will say, "Oh! Look! God is smiling down on us again." When the sun finally comes out fully, we often see a rainbow. The beauty of the rainbow after the storm has passed reminds us of God's promise not to destroy us.

Just as we can see God's hand in the power of the storm, the lightning, and the beautiful rainbow, so, too have we seen his hand at work through our valley of depression. He has sent light to dawn across the valley and to show us a new day.

That one weekend in California when Dr. Dobson, Dr. John Townsend, and Sealy Yates all pointed us toward help came like lightning—God's direction was so striking and clear-cut. I had headed for California under a cloud of depression, engulfed in my own dark pain, but the way God intervened struck me as a brilliant display of his power and love toward me.

The progressive effects of counseling were not striking but more like those beautiful rays of sunlight that came and went, illuminating the landscape for a moment, then passing. My life remained overcast to varying degrees for several years after the crisis—from the time we were in Ohio in March 1990 until Dave's amputation in June 1991 and on into our time in Colorado, well into 1994. The ongoing counseling caused the light of understanding to break through at various times to help me see clearly areas where I needed to change.

When my first counselor brought to light the pain I had avoided for so long, it hurt. That was why I quit going after several sessions; I wanted immediate relief. Although the counselor was offering to help me go through the pain and gain understanding along the way, I didn't want to go through the necessary process or take the time to see where I needed to change. I wanted the counselor to fix me, but I had to accept that I had to go through the pain to get past it. When I shied away because of the discomfort, the depression came over me again.

When I went back into counseling, I gradually accepted that I must learn a new way of looking at life. That was when I grew to appreciate each ray of light that broke through my confusion and depression.

In sharing a few of my experiences in counseling, I hope to demystify the experience and show you how counseling helped me find joy again. These are random moments that stand out in my memory as times when the light came through and I was able to adjust my approach to life in ways that helped me.

In one meeting, Dr. Townsend asked me, "Jan, how are your friendships?"

"I have a ton of friends. Nothing is wrong with my friendships." I told him confidently.

His next question stopped me in my tracks, "I'm sure you do, Jan, but of all your friendships, how many of those friends need you?"

"Well, they all need me in one way or another. What's wrong with that?"

He answered my question with another question. "How many of those same friends do you need?"

"Well," I paused as I started to see what he was getting at. "None."

"So in all your friendships you are the one always helping them, never the other way around?"

I thought about his statement. When we were in baseball, I had peer relationships with other baseball wives. I didn't have to worry about ulterior motives people might have in being my friend. So I had a network of balanced support through which we helped each other. After baseball, I gravitated toward relationships where I felt needed. This gave me some sense of security that people wouldn't leave me if I continued to help them. While this sounds very "Christian" in theory, in reality it became exhausting and ultimately destructive.

The counseling helped me look at my relationships with new criteria. When I moved to Colorado, I consciously tried to balance my relationships so that I developed a group of friends who were peers, who needed me as much as I needed them. I realize now that I am not meant to be the saving grace of every person I meet who has a need, and I acknowledge my limitations so that I am cautious about any relationship where the need is only one-sided. The book

Safe People, by Henry Cloud and John Townsend, has also helped me clarify how to develop and maintain healthy relationships.

Another issue I dealt with is how I handled confrontation. This dawned on me early in the counseling process, but it has taken a long time to see growth in this area. It happened in an early session with Dr. Sommers back in Ohio. He was initially getting to know me, asking general questions about how I approached different situations. I had read enough counseling books to be a little smug in my understanding of the terminology and savvy about giving the answers I thought would be the right ones.

He said, "Tell me how you deal with confronting people when that becomes necessary."

"Oh, I'm good at confrontation." I assured him.

"Really," Dr. Sommers said, nodding me on. "Give me an example of a time you needed to confront someone and how you did it."

"Well, I can't think of a particular example because I do it all the time. Whenever anyone is mad at me or displeased with me, I go to them immediately and make it right. I ask them what I did to make them angry, then I take care of the problem, whatever it is."

His expression clouded over. "Okay, but what do you do to confront someone when you are angry or you are the one who has been wronged?"

"Well . . ." I paused because I was stunned by the question. I had never even considered confronting anyone who hurt or mistreated me. "In those cases, I don't do anything. I just ignore it or play it down until it doesn't seem like it matters anymore."

"Jan," Dr. Sommers said gently, "you are not confronting in a healthy way when you rush after anyone who is displeased with you to find out what you must do to keep that person from being mad at you. A big difference exists between placating someone and being a peacemaker. Ignoring situations where you have been wronged just because you don't want to make waves reveals a problem. You need to learn how to live honestly with others, not just do whatever they want so they don't get mad at you."

I sat there stunned. This was an area of my life that I thought was fine. In light of what his questions revealed, I suddenly had to reevaluate the pattern of all my relationships and consider what that pattern meant. The understanding I gained set me free to see situations differently and respond differently. I still find it a challenge to confront someone when I feel mistreated, but now I realize it as a good thing to do, and I am learning how to do it better and better as I grow.

Before, I just stuffed my complaints and pretended to be fine, while I seethed inside. Now if I catch myself seething whenever I am around a person, I stop to examine why I'm seething. If I've been wronged or sinned against, I go to the person as Scripture tells us to in Matthew 18:15–17. I still have to swallow hard before confronting those who might get mad at me or retreat from me. Courage is required for me to confront others when it is necessary, but at least I realize confrontation is necessary at times to keep relationships balanced and honest.

Before this counseling session, I had prided myself on my graciousness shown in overlooking wrongs against me. I saw my placating and people-pleasing-at-all-costs kind of behavior as a virtue when it really wasn't. Only when I was weakened by depression, could I see my life in a new light and take steps in a new direction.

Dave and I didn't go to counseling for marriage problems, but while we were in counseling together, we saw our relationship in a new light that helped us improve our communication. This made our marriage better than ever.

For instance, I had a tendency to back away from an issue if it kindled Dave's anger. I hated it whenever Dave got mad at me, so I would go to great lengths to keep him from getting angry. I accepted this pattern without examining it. One time a situation arose where I had agreed to do something with another person that would inconvenience our family. I agreed because I didn't want to hurt the other person's feelings, but this time my placating would impact Dave, too. He didn't like it one bit and was angry that I had agreed. Dave and I were arguing about this in the car on the way to a counseling session. The argument escalated as we neared the counselor's office and Dave said to me, "And we are *not* going to discuss this with the counselor."

Well, it didn't take a Ph.D. in psychology to tell that something was wrong between us when we settled into our chairs in the counselor's office. The tension was obvious—the body language was carrying on the argument without words.

The counselor said, "Does anyone want to tell me what's going on?"

I looked at Dave questioningly. He glared at me. And I told the counselor the whole story about the argument and how Dave told me not to say anything.

He asked Dave, "Is that true?"

Dave nodded sheepishly. "Yeah."

We didn't need to pretend, so Dave proceeded to explain his view of the problem. Then the counselor asked me to explain my view of the problem. He offered insight about how each of us related to the other and helped us recognize legitimate concerns on each side. He pointed out the issues to be discussed and helped us stay focused on the issue at hand. Had we not been with the counselor, we would have been so busy defending our respective positions that we wouldn't have been able to hear or understand each other.

One of the primary benefits of being in counseling together was that I felt safe to discuss issues in front of the counselor that I might have avoided for fear that they would arouse Dave's anger. The counselor helped us diffuse the anger and get to the real issues. He didn't take anyone's side. Instead, he helped us hear what the other was trying to say. Before we entered counseling, an argument like the one in the car would have come to an impasse. Then we would have endured two or three days of angry silence until one of us broke down and started talking again. But that pattern never resulted in either of us gaining understanding of the issues at the heart of the conflict. With the counselor's help, we identified the problem, saw the patterns of behavior that caused the conflict, and worked together to deal with our shared problems. That has revolutionized how we relate to each other and how we respond to life together.

I understand how Christians can be skeptical about the emphasis some people put on using a counselor as a substitute for seeking wisdom from God, but none of our Christian counselors ever led us away from seeking God's wisdom. Instead, they shared the godly wisdom they had gained with us while they taught us to examine our lives to make sure we were living the balanced life God would have us live. The Bible encourages us to seek out wisdom and search for understanding as one would search for hidden treasure. That's what we were doing in seeking godly counsel. Without the understanding we gained, we would not have made the changes that have helped us come out of depression.

The counselors also helped us recognize and accept our weaknesses. Weakness caused us to turn to God for the wisdom we needed to make good decisions. I found that when I asked God for his wisdom and expected it to come, it always came, sometimes through a counselor, sometimes through a friend, sometimes through books that spoke directly to our situation.

For instance, I found tremendous wisdom and comfort from reading about others who went through adversity in life. One book called *They Found the Secret* tells stories of effective Christians who discovered that the secret key of suffering and adversity is what unlocks the door to intimacy with God and useful service in God's kingdom. That encouraged me to approach our suffering and adversity with hope instead of despair.

Another ray of light came to me from the seventeenth-century writings of Fenelon. His letters were written to encourage Christians being persecuted for their faith in the court of Louis XIV. I was astounded at how his words, written hundreds of years ago, spoke directly to my condition. He writes in Letter 10:

> Though it sounds strange to say it, I'm rejoicing that God has reduced you to a state of weakness. Your ego can neither be convinced or forced into submission by any other means. It is always finding secret lines of supply from your courage. It is always finding impenetrable retreats in your own cleverness. It was hidden from your eyes while it fed upon the subtle poison of an apparent generosity, as you constantly sacrificed yourself for others. But now God has forced it to cry aloud; To come forth into open day and display its excessive jealousy. Oh, how painful but how beneficial are these times of weakness.

I felt as though he had written this to me, and he didn't even know me! God used this insight along with those I was gaining from counseling to show me that bending over backward to keep everybody happy was not good. It was a subtle poison; as I constantly sacrificed myself for others, ignoring my own legitimate needs, I was killing myself. This understanding helped me check myself and my motives so that I could realign my priorities in a healthy way.

I cannot say that a moment came when I was healed in an instant and immediately came out of the valley. My body was depressed, and it took time to fully recover. Recovery was a gradual process, not the instant cure I had hoped for. As I healed, I began to experience moments of joy again.

One night, when I was tucking Jonathan into bed, I looked at him, and a warm, wonderful feeling of love returned. *Oh, my baby!* I thought.

Then I thought, *Oh my ... I felt! I had a warm feeling ... That's a feeling I haven't had in so long!*

I was impatient that it took so long to start feeling better, but my doctor explained it to me like this: "It took years, Jan, to get you to the point that caused you to crash. Do you think that you're going to get well automatically? No! It's going to take time."

I remember seeing Dr. Townsend after Dave's amputation, two months after our first meeting. I said, "I'm beginning to have some good days."

He replied, "That's exciting!" And he went on to say that he would have been worried if I had told him I was doing wonderfully. He assured me that the path of healing I was on was the right one.

Today I am out of the depression. But I learned for myself that the path out of the valley of depression is slow and laborious. From the time of my first panic attack in 1990, it took me over five years to recover, and I can't tell how long I was depressed before I had to face up to it and find help. Many times, storm clouds rolled over the mountains and drenched me in showers of tears. Many times, I almost missed the beams of hope gleaming through the black clouds.

But in the mountains, after the storms pass, the air is fresh, the sky, a clear translucent blue. Wildflowers that were watered by the rains paint the fields with brilliant colors as far as the eye can see. Like Solomon, I can say, "See! The winter is past; the rains are over and gone. Flowers appear on the earth; the season of singing has come."

That is what I see in my life now: a fresh newness, a springlike beauty and joy. Through the valleys of depression and the storms of tears, the promises of God have proven true in my life:

> Those who sow in tears
> will reap with songs of joy.
> He who goes out weeping,
> carrying seed to sow,
> will return with songs of joy,
> carrying sheaves with him. (Psalm 126:5–6)

Seventeen

Blessed Are Those Who Mourn

*O*ne of the insights I gained in counseling was on the importance of mourning. Little did I know that this insight would
not only lead to my healing but also lead Dave and me to a totally
new career.

"There will come a time, Jan, when you are going to have to
go back and grieve," Dr. Sommers calmly explained during one of
our regular counseling sessions in the fall of 1992. "Grieving is a
normal and necessary part of moving out of depression. Even the
Bible says that there is "a time to weep and a time to laugh, a time
to mourn and a time to dance."

"Well, that's fine and dandy for you to tell me to grieve," I
replied, "but I don't feel like crying now. How do I grieve? I've
never grieved anything in my life. I've stuffed everything."

"You mean to tell me that you never think of your mom and
dad or what's happened to Dave and feel sad?"

"Well, yeah, I feel sad."

"Well, what do you do when you feel sad, Jan?"

"I just change the subject; I think of something else."

"Jan, the next time you have that feeling of sadness, stop! I want you to stay there. Don't change the subject. Don't leave that place of sadness. Stay there and allow yourself to feel whatever feelings arise."

I agreed to try. I can't say that I went back home and miraculously allowed myself to feel the pain. But a month and a half later, I was upstairs in the guest room, wrapping Christmas presents for the kids. This brought back thoughts of other Christmas seasons. One of my favorite parts of Christmas was choosing just the right gift for my parents. How I looked forward to watching them open their gifts! But I would never be able to give them another Christmas present again.

When that thought came to me, my first instinct was to run to get the children and cheer myself up. Then I recalled my doctor's voice saying, "Stop!" So I stopped and simply allowed myself to feel what I was feeling. I started to cry, and I cried for a long time. I didn't just cry; I wailed, feeling the sorrow from the tips of my toes to the top of my head. I must have cried like that for at least ten minutes or more before it naturally subsided. After I was done I felt lighter; it had a cleansing effect on me. Crying felt so good that I wondered why I had avoided it for all these years.

A short time later, I was driving to the cleaners, taking Dave's suits to be altered. We get the left sleeve cut off and have a shoulder built in, so the suit fits smoothly and doesn't look awkward on his body. I happened to look over at the suits hanging there in the car and thought about what I was doing. I thought not only about the sleeve that was about to be cut off, but I thought about the arm that used to be in that sleeve, and I felt sad. I thought about the shoulder I used to lean on, the shoulder that was now gone.

I could have turned up the radio or tried to think about something else, but I didn't. I allowed myself to feel the sadness of my loss. I had lost Dave's arm, too; with his amputation I lost the arms that used to hold me, the hand on which he wore his wedding ring, the hand that held mine when we were dating in high school. As I allowed myself to feel the deep sense of loss and sadness over losing Dave's arm, tears blurred my vision, and I sobbed as I drove down the freeway. I stayed with the sadness until it ran its course, and again I felt a good strong sense of relief that came from allowing the sadness to flow out with my tears.

As for Dave, he initially tried not to grieve. Instead, he denied his loss by busying himself helping others and only looking on the bright side. So he, too, ended up in his own bout with depression several months after the amputation. His depression lifted only when he learned to grieve by acknowledging how much he missed baseball and his former lifestyle. For him, grieving was a systematic process of itemizing each loss, admitting how much it meant to him, and allowing himself to mourn in his own way. He grieved the major losses, such as losing his arm and career, as well as the smaller losses, such as no longer being able to tie his own shoes. Once he worked through these losses, the depression lifted.

During this time of learning to grieve, we continued to receive letters from people who related to Dave's story because they were suffering something similar. We fully expected the mail to slack off as the media attention died down, but it never slowed. Our publisher had paid Insight for Living to answer the initial influx of mail that had overwhelmed me, but when it became apparent that the flow of mail wasn't letting up, we hired two women to answer correspondence from our home office.

Dave also continued speaking and visiting cancer patients, amputees, and their families. Ever since the Giants had invited us back to Candlestick Park for "Dave Dravecky Day" on October 5, 1991, Dave had enjoyed encouraging others. On "Dave Dravecky Day," he invited several children who were amputees and cancer survivors to join him on the mound, calling them the real heroes. All along, he responded to requests to make phone calls to people in cancer wards, to comfort family members who had lost loved ones, and to compare notes with other amputees on life after such a loss. All of this seemed to fill a real need and brought Dave great joy.

Dave and I had always appreciated Oswald Chambers' book *My Utmost for His Highest*. One of his devotions reminded us of the shared vision God had given us—that vision of August 15, 1989, when Dave fell from the mound and we shared a sense of expectancy over what wonderful things God would do next in our lives.

Oswald writes:

God gives us a vision, and then He takes us down to the valley to batter us into the shape of that vision. It is in the valley that so many of us give up and faint. Every God-given vision will become real if we will only have patience. Just think of the enormous amount of free time God has! He is never in a hurry. Yet we are always in such a frantic hurry. While still in the light of the glory of the vision, we go right out to do things, but the vision is not yet real in us. God has to take us into the valley and put us through fires and floods to batter us into shape, until we get to the point where He can trust us with the reality of the vision. Ever since God gave us the vision, He has been at work. He is getting us into the shape of the goal He has for us, and yet over and over again we try to escape from the Sculptor's hand in an effort to batter ourselves into the shape of our own goal.

This devotion stopped me in my tracks. God certainly had been battering us into shape. And we certainly were trying to shape our own goals! We kept trying to pursue a career in baseball with no success. Perhaps God was trying to tell us something.

I thought about our situation further. Our connections with baseball had started to fade, but letters continued to pour in from people who suffered from cancer and amputation. Could this be an indication of God's vision for us?

I went to Dave to share my thoughts.

"Hey, don't you see what's happening?" I asked him. "Maybe God is closing all the doors in baseball because he has something else for you to do."

The more we talked, the more we realized a stark contrast between the career paths we had been considering and the one God might be leading us toward. A line of people were clamoring to minister to pro baseball players, but few people had a heart to encourage and minister to cancer patients and amputees.

"Dave," I asked, "tell me this. Do you have a sense of joy when you work with a cancer patient or encourage a grieving family?"

"Yes!" A smile crept across Dave's face as he realized that God may have already been showing us what we were supposed to be doing.

"Is there anyone else doing a national Christian ministry to bring encouragement to cancer patients, amputees, and their families?"

Dave just grinned.

Together we came to the realization that we were uniquely suited to comfort others with the comfort we had received from God. Instead of closing up shop in response to the letters we received, we geared up. We opened an office for Dave Dravecky's Outreach of Hope in the summer of 1993, after our move to Colorado. The mission of our ministry is "Offering hope and encouragement through Jesus Christ to those suffering from cancer or amputation."

We provide encouraging books, tapes, and materials along with comfort for those who have been through similar episodes of suffering. We make calls to those referred to us, produce a newsletter called *The Encourager*, and send out gift baskets of practical and spiritual help. We didn't set out with this mission in mind; God led us here.

When we told people what we were going to do, some said, "Why would you choose to do something like that? Why would you choose to work with people who are sick and dying? It's so depressing all the time." But it's not depressing for us, and that's why God can use us in this work. We enjoy comforting others because we know how much it meant for us to be comforted when we were going through the ravages of cancer. We also give others a place where they can comfort others after they have been through the valley themselves. Helping others is a therapeutic way our volunteers work through their own pain and loss in a meaningful way.

We continue to make plans to expand our work to meet the needs that come to our attention every day. Our dream is to provide a curriculum to churches and teach them how to care for their cancer patients and amputees or those going through adversity. Churches that have a cancer support group have a unique opportunity to share the gospel with people who are eager to hear about the hope of heaven.

We're not interested in having Dave Dravecky Ministries all over the United States. Rather we would like to teach and encourage churches to come alongside those who are suffering from cancer in their congregation and community.

Cancer can be a long disease. It can go on for years and years. Initially, people surround you, but then one by one they often drop off. The majority of people who have cancer find out who their friends really are. Many cancer victims suffer drastic physical changes: Many lose their hair, and many are very thin. Their physical changes and possible impending death reminds people of their own mortality, so people stay away.

But our ministry encourages people to stay close, to support, to comfort through caring and touch. Yes, touch. Most people don't like to touch cancer victims for fear of hurting them, but touch is an important part of letting people know that you care. We encourage those suffering with cancer with something as simple as a touch of kindness.

Surprisingly, even though I am now in a ministry where I'm constantly reminded that death is a possibility, I'm not depressed anymore. Being in this ministry actually changes my perspective on my own life in a positive way, for I am constantly reminded to live with an eternal perspective. I know that whatever happens to me down here isn't as important as what I will see in eternity, and I am reminded time and again that we are all just passing through.

In his book *When God Doesn't Make Sense,* Dr. James Dobson says, "It blows me away that all of these people are sick, dying, all these tragedies happen. Yet, when the tragedy hits your family, people say, 'Why me?' Why not? It's going to hit you sometime. Why be surprised?"

Scripture tells me that I should expect to suffer; in fact, it says, "Consider it pure joy, my brothers, when you face trials of many kinds, because you know that the testing of your faith develops perseverance. Perseverance must finish its work in you so that you may be mature and complete, not lacking anything" (James 1:2–4). God says he allows suffering and trials to mature us; but you don't often hear that message.

It is far more common to hear people give a pep talk to those who are suffering. People who are hurting often come to us and report, "Well, people have told me if I will just read the Bible more or go to church more, I will be freed from this pain." Over and over we counsel Christians who are surprised by having to face suffering, because they were led to believe it wouldn't happen to them. If the person who's suffering did read the Bible more, they might come to realize that suffering is part of life in a fallen world. Instead they are told, "Just read the Bible more," as though the act of Bible reading will make all the pain go away. That teaching is contrary to Scripture.

Instead of giving them a pep talk, those who want to help others who are suffering need only to share their sorrow. We are commanded as Christians to weep with those who weep. I used to be one of those who never wanted people to cry. I'd change the

subject or try to cheer them up. It makes me sad to realize that I
didn't help them by doing so. Now, I don't change the subject anymore; I listen to their stories. I stand beside them, I cry with them,
I hold their hands. I can't relieve the pain, but I know there's no
way to get on the other side of the pain except to go through it. I
have learned that those who mourn will be comforted, so I let them
mourn. I even encourage it. Now I understand that mourning is a
necessary part of dealing with loss. It is not a weakness in faith.

I am amazed at what God had to take me through to change
me from being one who would find good reason to avoid pain and
suffering to someone who is able to comfort those who are suffering. He had to take each of us through a tremendous amount of
pain to prepare us for this ministry of comfort. He had to change
my heart. I don't know exactly how he did it or when he did it, but
I can tell you where he did it—in the valley of suffering. We didn't
orchestrate any of this; we didn't even welcome it at the time. We
who have known the fellowship of suffering join the ranks of all
those other Christians I read about who became useful to God
through the things that they suffered.

There is a time to mourn, and we must remember that mourning takes differing amounts of time for different people. Leslie is a
good example of this point.

Leslie came to us with her husband, Jim, the summer of 1994
when he was dying from melanoma. When Jim died, he was only
forty years old, and he left Leslie with three boys. It has been eight
months since Jim died. Leslie now works as a volunteer with our
ministry, and she is beginning to comfort others with the comfort
she received from us. But she is still grieving. She still cries, and
she's starting to feel like we're probably all thinking, "Get over it
already, Leslie," which some of her friends have said to her. I had
to reassure her that we know from experience that grief gets worse
before it gets better. She was relieved to hear that.

Leslie's husband had battled cancer for seven years, and there
was always a great deal of uncertainty about when and how he was

going to die. When death did come, it was so beautiful and peaceful that it was a relief to have the uncertainty over. But as time went on, Leslie started to miss him like she had never dreamed possible. While the world just went on, forgetting the sadness of his death, Leslie's grief grew worse. Just recently, one of Leslie's friends said to her, "I think you need to take a more positive outlook. You need to get over this and go on with your life."

Leslie expressed a feeling that often keeps people from grieving fully. She said, "I hate to burden people. I'm such a downer to be around. I'd rather just stay to myself so no one has to be burdened with my grief."

Yes, I hated to be a burden, too; but I knew that what Leslie was going through was a normal part of what she has to go through. Grief is a burden meant to be shared. I said, "We've only known you the way you are, and we love you the way you are. Even in your sorrow, you're a joy to be around. We love being around you. Can you imagine, after you get through all this, what it's going to be like? To us, it will be like opening a surprise gift. We love you the way you are now. Can you imagine the additional gift that we're going to get when you finally come out of all of this?"

"But I feel like I should be past this," she said.

"Look," I told her, "we're your friends, and we love you. We're going to be here for you regardless of how long it takes or whether someone says you should be through it by now. We accept you the way you are."

We are not to judge how people suffer; we are to love them. We teach the people at our ministry that there is no proper way to suffer. Suffering is not tidy, because suffering is a purifying process, a process of cleansing out impurities. When suffering causes impurities to rise to the surface, naturally we are going to see the worst of people. Their selfishness is going to come out, their wrong priorities are going to become apparent, and they are not going to be able to mask their sinfulness anymore.

Suffering breaks down the walls that people put up to hide what's really inside. When you suffer, you can't keep up the nice facade. Dave, for example, could usually look like a good person. He could praise the Lord and say, "I know God's going to work all things together for good," but the more the heat was turned up, the less he was able to keep up the facade. All that was left was what was inside, and when what was inside of both of us came out, we were appalled and ashamed.

There's no right way to suffer. When I am talking with a mother whose child is dying of cancer, it does no good to say, "Don't feel sad," or "Don't be angry at God." There is no point in saying, "You shouldn't feel that way." If she feels that way, she feels that way. One who is suffering needs to deal with reality, not pretend to feel how someone else wants them to feel. Feelings are not right or wrong; but it is wrong to lie about how you feel. And you're no less of a Christian if you express those human emotions that come to the surface when you suffer, even if they are less than ideal. To me, you're more of a Christian because you are being honest, not donning some false front. Those who honestly face the depth of their suffering will recognize their need for God.

We should be allowed to be real, but that's not what typically happens. What do we say to ourselves when we see the purifying process of suffering at work in our lives? We say, *What's wrong with me? Why do I have these awful feelings? Why do I doubt God? Oh, my, look at me: I lose my temper, I become ugly, I scream, I swear, I throw things. I do all these terrible things.* Yet this is part of the process that causes us to fall on the mercy of God, which is where we will find the source of all comfort.

If you give in to the belief that you "should" suffer nicely, you will find yourself not only dealing with all of the anger and impurities within you but also dealing with the guilt that you shouldn't react in a less than "Christian" way. So, the more you try to handle it "the way you should," the more frustration and pain you develop within. If you fall into this cycle, you become one unbelievable time bomb. I think this is why we see more and more Christians in depression. When people aren't allowed to grieve honestly, they don't get through the grief; they get stuck in it! I think it's far better to go through the grief and let all the impurities come to the surface, then give them over to God along with all your doubts, fears, and unanswered questions. All of this is part of moving past the grief to the blessing that God promises to all who mourn.

Let me warn you away from one other trap that comes with the territory of grieving. It's the trap of comparing your grief with that of others. A woman came up to me after I spoke and said, "Well, I can see how you got through it. All you lost was your husband's arm. *I* lost my husband." I heard another woman console herself by saying, "I could have handled it if God just took my husband, but I lost two children to cancer."

No one wins when you try to compare your grief and loss with that of others. When my dad tried to stop my grief at the loss of my mother by comparing it with his loss, that did not help me at all. Loss is loss; it needs to be dealt with, and making comparisons doesn't help anyone.

One woman called and left a message for Dave saying, "I want to come back to God, but I'm so angry. Look at how unfair God was to me. You were cured of your cancer, but God allows my suffering to continue. How can I forgive him?"

Dave didn't call this woman, because she wouldn't have been comforted by Dave. She was convinced that God favored him, and her envy would have kept her from being comforted. Instead, Dave had Leslie call. She could relate to this woman because she, too, had experienced feelings that life had been unfair.

We have kept in touch with this woman. Her struggles still continue, but God has orchestrated several elements in her life to work together with Leslie's comfort to make life more bearable for her. Within a few weeks this woman came back to the Lord. Three weeks later, her husband also accepted Christ. All this simply because we ministered to her, listening to her in her needs.

Leslie said afterward, "You know, sometimes I feel so stupid when I explain to people what we do, because it seems so little, but it makes such a big difference."

What do we do? We care! We make regular calls, checking up on those who are grieving. We send our newsletter, *The Encourager.* We keep in touch with people after a loved one's death, including calling on the anniversary date of the death, remembering that the pain's still there.

If you have pain in your heart over a loss, don't be embarrassed; don't let anyone pressure you to get through it and get on with your life. If you have the pain of loss, don't stuff it down and avoid it; experience it, but don't experience it alone. Reach out to receive comfort from someone who has been through it. Then, in time, you, too, will be able to comfort others with the comfort you receive from God.

Eighteen

I Feel Just Like You!

I occasionally speak for women's groups, although this has been a rare event since I went through my bout with depression. I don't see myself as a teacher. What I usually do when I address a group of women is share much of what I have shared in this book. I see myself as an encourager to women to let them know they are not alone, especially those who are beaten down and discouraged by adversity in life.

In my speeches, I try to dispel false expectations of how the Christian life works. But when I arrived one weekend to speak at a women's conference, I was faced with a delicate problem. The planners had a beautiful event planned for five hundred women, about one hundred of whom did not know Jesus as Savior, and they wanted me to help them paint a lovely picture of what God would do for those who accept him.

I sensed that these women might not realize the focus of my message. The leaders were very polite to me, but they had stringent guidelines. I could understand their need to have some boundaries, but the woman in control wanted to know every little detail about what I was going to say. She had already sent me all the information on my guidelines in the mail, but she made a point to call me again to make sure I had read them. She seemed completely driven by these guidelines, so much so that I felt there was little room for the Holy Spirit to lead what I would say.

Before I stepped up to speak, the leaders told me, "We want you to ask for the women to make a commitment to Christ. You can have them write down their commitment to accept Christ on these little cards."

I thought, *Oh, my, what am I doing here? I'm not an evangelist.*

I smiled and nodded and tried to explain what I felt comfortable doing at the close of my talk. "I don't usually call for just a commitment to accept Christ," I told them. "I call for the women to acknowledge if they have areas of their lives that are troubling them, areas where they need to confess weakness, fear . . ."

My voice trailed off as the stunned and puzzled looks on their faces told me that they didn't like what I was saying.

Bravely, I continued, "I ask the women if there are areas where they need to let go and trust God, those areas where God may be leading them to a deeper walk, to deal with issues they may have been ignoring. Then I encourage them to ask for prayer. Actually, commitment to Christ is not normally in my plan. I see myself as more of an encourager rather than an evangelist."

The leader spoke up calmly, "If you won't ask for a simple commitment to Christ, you had better leave out everything because when you ask for a recommitment or stir up these other areas of difficulty, nonbelievers only become confused."

I thought, *Oh, heaven forbid we might lead someone to think that something could go wrong after you accept Christ. What am I doing here? What I have to share is in total antithesis to what these people want. They want "I accepted Christ and lived happily ever after." Oh, Lord, what am I going to do?*

I knew what I had to do. I had to tell them what I knew to be true from my life and from the Bible.

So I gave a shortened testimony of my life. I told the audience how I felt for many years as if I were in a boxing match: I would get hit and then I'd get up by my own strength. Then another blow would come, I'd go down, and then I'd force myself up again.

I shared about wanting to turn back to the world, about shaking my fist at God and wanting to flee him. I talked about the confusion of wondering if I really believed what I claim to believe. I said, "You get to a point where you can't do it anymore. You simply can't be the ideal image of a Christian. But the American packaged version of Christianity is designed to make you feel that you just don't measure up if you're not happy and healthy and rich! It's like those beauty magazine ads that promise, 'Use this moisturizer and you will look years younger'! But happiness and riches aren't what Christianity is about. It simply doesn't match with what life throws at us!"

When these women heard me saying that I couldn't keep up the facade or keep pretending that the contents matched the picture on the Christian package, they weren't confused; they were relieved! A number of women came up to me afterward and said they had felt like I had felt—many times! I was relieved that I didn't have to pretend that Christianity is something it is not.

In the end, I was glad that I didn't hide my struggles, because I found that by sharing my struggles, I helped many other women who were hiding theirs. One of the women at this event wrote me a letter to tell me her story. She wrote, in part:

Dear Jan,

Wow! After last weekend, I feel like I used to after coming home from church camp . . . high, high, high! I was really ready to walk away from everything that represented Christianity in my life because I just couldn't measure up anymore; I had lost sight of my Jesus. The past two years have been full of crisis and transition; so much so that I plummeted into a dark depression about six months ago. Although I'm recovering slowly, there are still many days when the darkness swallows up any light, and I sit hopeless and confused. This all began when I said good-bye to my protector and best friend here on earth, my dad. He suffered with cancer for five years and then left us at age fifty-six. Shortly thereafter we went through a grueling church split that left me reeling spiritually. Two months later, a good friend of ours died of cancer in his mid-thirties, and a month after that my dear sweet grand-mother died suddenly. Shortly after that my husband's grandmother died, and to top it all off, we then found we were losing our job of eight years and had to relocate.

She went on to tell me a few more traumatic episodes that had happened in the same time period. Then she continued:

I know you must hear many people's stories. I really didn't intend to tell you mine. But I wanted you to know a little of where I've been so you would know how deeply you affected my life with your testimony. You see, I've been suffering from fear of illness and dying. I have severe panic attacks and can hardly drag myself out of bed each day for fear of when and how it will strike and how long I have to live after it does. I've been in counseling, but it still seems to be such a long process with progress and regres-sion seeming to stay balanced so I never really move for-ward. And what so struck me about your testimony is that I am a *controller!* The Lord continually reminds me to *let go!* I suppose the way to get that point across is to allow circumstances beyond our control. But I still try to con-trol the uncontrollable. I could go on, Jan, but I only wanted to say a heartfelt thank-you for your sensitivity to the Spirit. I had been praying for direction and confirmation in many areas before I attended the conference, and so much came through your testimony. I'm learning that all we have is Jesus. It sounds really good to talk about spiritual things, but when the unsettling circumstances of life set in, all the religion and works accounted for nothing; I had to press in and find a friend, the Lord and Savior that I really had never known before, although Christianity has been a way of life for me since I was a child. It really is *grace*, isn't it? It really is *him*, isn't it? If only we could grasp what he really intends for us—wow!

With tears still in my eyes when I think about your testimony and what it continues to mean to me, I thank you again for allowing the Lord to use you and your pain for his glory in spreading love to others. Until he comes . . .

This letter and many others like it assured me that many women feel just like me but are hiding the pain because they think that is the "Christian" thing to do.

Shortly thereafter, I spoke at Mothers of Preschoolers International (MOPS). There I saw a crowd of women who looked just as I had looked about ten years ago. They seemed to have it all together and were so eager to do the right thing. They all looked pretty, well-dressed, and energetic. In them I saw a younger version of me, the woman who wanted to be everything and do everything the right way.

When I shared my story, I was surprised to learn that many of these women were dealing with panic attacks and had never told anyone. The woman in charge was extremely attractive, the "cheerleader" and homecoming-queen type. She seemed extremely capable, but she had recently resigned her position because she was not capable of doing everything.

When I came home, I received a letter from the MOPS leader. She wrote:

Dear Jan,

There were many women that felt like I did after your talk today—incredibly thankful, touched by the Holy Spirit through you, and no longer alone. Though I cannot speak for the others specifically, I would like to tell you thank-you so much for being so open and trusting with us—especially about having wanted to leave God and go back to the world. Sometimes I start to think that, and then I become fearful that I'll really make God mad, so I erase the thought quickly and trudge forward. The losses you've experienced and struggles you and your family have endured have truly served you well. Though I could feel your pain and anguish, I was so thankful that God lifted you up through all of it in order to share his love with others.

You're Jan Dravecky, and I'm just me, but you made me feel like we were so close—like I could tell you anything, and you truly would care. Anyway, when you talked about the panic attacks, I knew God had arranged your being with us today! For no conscious reason, I experienced a panic attack driving over a bridge one and a half years ago. This was a road I've crossed probably two thousand times, at least. I tried to make myself get over it many times, but the racing heart, numb legs, and dizziness was always there, and I even started waking up at night thinking about it. So for over a year, I have avoided that bridge.

I, too, grew up in a good church-going family and really didn't know Christ personally until a few years ago. I have tried to figure out if these attacks are from Satan, and if so, why? Why isn't my faith working? I finally reached the conclusion that I couldn't fix this problem and went to a Christian counselor yesterday for the first time ever. Your being there today and sharing so much was a gift from God. I felt such a sense of hope and anticipation to see how God will use this in me for his purpose. Maybe God is trying to teach me to let go all the way, too. I do believe he'll be there to catch me, though sometimes it's hard to believe.

In the spring of 1995, I spoke for a women's retreat in Dallas. I gave my testimony about how God took me through the valley and brought me out to experience a sense of joy I'd never known before. I also spoke about our hope of heaven and how that can help us conquer fear.

After I spoke Friday night, the woman heading the retreat came to me and said, "Jan, I have a woman I think you need to talk to." She then introduced me to Rhonda, a thirty-six-year-old mother of two children. Rhonda poured out her story.

An extremely attractive, competent, and intelligent woman, Rhonda didn't lean on people easily. Recently she had been diagnosed with a potentially fatal connective-tissue disease. She had started chemotherapy treatment and suffered constant pain. Her husband really wanted to support her and had a sincere desire to be there for her, but he just didn't seem to know how to demonstrate his concern.

That very morning of the night we met, Rhonda had decided to commit suicide and had a plan to do so. She was driving everyone away from her. She wrote a note to her close friend and told her that she didn't want her friendship anymore. That friend dropped by that afternoon and did not abandon Rhonda even after she tried to push her away. Her friend's faithfulness kept Rhonda from killing herself. Her friend said, "You can't push me out of your life," and sat and cried with her. Another woman had invited Rhonda to come hear me speak, and she decided to come give it a try. When she heard my testimony, she knew God had intervened to bring her to the meeting. She asked to speak with me afterward.

For a long time, all I did was listen to her, caring for her and identifying with her struggles. She told me how she hated burdening her friends with her problems.

She said, "I told my doctor that I was withdrawing from people and feeling really down, and all he said was, 'Maybe you just need to be alone.'"

She didn't want to go to counseling because she thought it wouldn't help her. I said, "Rhonda, your problem is that you won't lean on people. You need people. I was like you, so self-sufficient. I had many friends, but my relationships were all one-way relationships. They needed me, but I didn't need them. I never needed anybody. I made sure I could take care of myself so I didn't have to depend on anyone else."

She looked at me and said, "That's how I feel, Jan."

I shared with her something I had read in a Minirth-Meier book. "Adam was in perfect union with God, but God looked at Adam and said, 'It's not good for you to be alone.' We are relational; we need one another."

But she told me, "I don't want to need anyone!"

We continued to talk until 1:00 in the morning. The next day Rhonda gave me this note:

Dear Jan:

I've never taken the word *friend* lightly . . . So I lie here and wonder, Jan, because after such a short time, I call you friend. But it was through God, through you, that my heart was touched and hope was given. There is a love within my heart for you. Once again I was able to open up to God. In the beginning it was only to say, "Thank you, God, for Jan." In his love and in my heart's prayers, I will always remember and think of you.

Rhonda was not the only one touched by my story. As I was speaking the next morning at the same church, I looked out in the audience, and most of the women were crying. One over here was sobbing, then another one over there was sobbing. After I finished speaking, I expected the tears to end.

Then the head of the women's retreat, the pastor's wife, asked if anyone had anything to share. Rhonda got up, sobbing, and told the group what she had told me the night before.

Then another woman got up and said: "I've been walking the halls of this church for twenty-six years, and I have never shared my pain or my secrets with anyone. But now is the time. My husband, whom you all know, is dying of a lung disease. He won't let anyone know he's dying because he is afraid to tell anyone he smokes cigarettes and can't quit. I know it's not right to smoke, but it's not right that a man who loves God and has been a faithful member of this church should die alone either. He's dying, and won't quit smoking or can't, and I'm tired of trying to keep up the image."

She just kept going, "I, too, want to control things; I want everyone to get along . . . I manipulate relationships . . ." on and on she went, pouring out her pain. Well, she was up there a long time confessing. After all, she had been holding it in for twenty-six years! She talked about trying to win approval by being what she thought others expected her to be. Then she looked at the pastor's wife and said, "I've wanted you to like me . . . I did! In all these years I have been working in this church; what do you think my motivation was? I wanted you to notice me. I wanted your approval . . . I wanted your affirmation. I wanted you to notice me and like me." She started sobbing.

The next woman that came up was an oncology nurse. She was the one who was to my left and sobbed through my entire talk. A go-getter and doer, she, too, started having panic attacks, but she refused to get help because she thought it was ungodly.

She almost didn't make it to the meeting because she can't drive, due to her panic attacks, but her husband said, "I'll drive you there." After she heard me talk, she stood up and said, "The reason that you're here is for me. I've been living with unspeakable terror, and I have not wanted to go for help. God brought you here to help me."

Then another girl got up and told how, when she was seven years old, her mother had been committed to the psychiatric ward and she just sobbed and sobbed. Another woman got up to share that her father was a pastor who had committed adultery. She had been trying to manipulate the family to get everybody back together, but her dad had left her mother and remarried. As I talked, the Lord revealed to her that she was manipulating all her relationships; she needed to take her hand off her father and allow God to deal with him. She needed to let her father pay the consequences of his sin.

Those are just a few of the women who spoke that day. They took turns pouring their hearts out. After each woman shared her story, we would stop and pray for her. Finally, the pastor's wife had to say, "We can only take one more." These women were being set free because they were able to share the truth. And the Lord allowed me to see the harvest, the firstfruits of what the Holy Spirit was doing in their hearts.

Just going through pain and sharing is not the end of the story. Love is the conclusion. When we reach out to each other in the midst of pain, we learn to give and receive love. I didn't stay stuck in the pain. I have come through it—and so can you.

Nineteen

Facing Off with Fear

*I*mmediately after the women's retreat, Dave and I flew home from Dallas. The weather that evening was worse than any I had ever seen. Two storm systems barreled into each other in the middle of Texas, and we flew right between them. I figured that they wouldn't let our plane take off if it wasn't safe, but I later learned that our flight was the last one to take off. All flights after ours were canceled because of the severe weather.

Everyone on the plane looked uneasy, exchanging wary glances. The flight attendants remained in their seats, holding onto the handrails provided for such occasions. The seat belt sign never went off, nor did anyone expect it to. Then the voice of the pilot came over the speakers. "Passengers, please tighten your seat belts." I knew what that meant; we were into some really heavy turbulence. Of all the flights we've taken, this was the first time we were told to *tighten* our seat belts. I took that to mean only one thing, *We're gonna be droppin'!*

My heart raced, but it wasn't a panic attack; this was normal, anybody-in-their-right-mind-would-be-afraid fear! The plane bounced and rolled though monstrous storm clouds. We came around one system and saw another coming. The pilot rolled the plane this way and that. We flew around Austin, and then went through another storm system. The whole time, I was thinking, *Lord, I just spent the whole weekend telling people about heaven and living as though we believe in eternity, and now I am scared to death. I don't want to drop out of the sky. Please, God, don't let us die like this!*

It was a humbling experience. I was being challenged: What did I really believe? If I believed in heaven, why was I terrified? Here I had just told three different groups to live as though they were on their way to heaven. Now I was flying through the clouds—about as close to heaven as one can get—and I was not focused on heaven. Instead I was downright scared.

That experience taught me an important lesson: Fear is part of the human condition. No wonder Jesus and the angels had to keep telling people over and over, "Don't be afraid." As human beings, we are prone to fear, no matter how much we believe in God or heaven. And the fear of death can hold tremendous power over us. God talks about our human condition in Hebrews 2:14–15: "Since the children have flesh and blood, he too shared in their humanity so that by his death [Jesus] might destroy him who holds the power of death—that is, the devil—and free those who all their lives were held in slavery by their fear of death."

God understands the fear common to all humanity. He isn't the author of death; he is the one who came to vanquish death. Death is the last enemy God will vanquish. When it comes to facing death, I am just like a child; I am just flesh and blood. Jesus understands because he took on our human condition to deal with the fear of death that has held me in slavery for much of my life.

My experience on the plane convinces me that I will have to face off with fear for the rest of my life, but I don't have to live in slavery to fear anymore. I have to admit that I believe in a mighty God, the resurrected Christ, who proved his power over the grave.

I also have to admit I'm still afraid on occasion. Now I am learning to admit my fears honestly to God, who understands my human condition.

When I was struggling with panic attacks and from bondage to fear, there were some actions that I found helpful in putting those fears to rest. It is my hope that these steps will help you if you have similar struggles.

1. Bring all your fears into the light of truth. Dealing with panic attacks has been one of the most terrifying experiences I have ever known. I am amazed at how many people with panic attacks try to keep it a secret. I don't think people like to talk about their panic attacks because it makes people think that they're mentally unstable. I have lived alone in that terror and fear, but I don't recommend staying there alone. Panic disorders can be caused by a variety of conditions, but if they are happening to you, they are real and should be dealt with. The first step is to stop hiding your condition.

2. Read good books that will help you identify what may be contributing to your condition, books like *Adrenaline and Stress* by Dr. Archibald Hart. Some panic attacks are fed by heightened fears and are aggravated by a release of adrenaline. The physical effects of that adrenaline surge—like a rapid heart rate—can scare you. When it scares you, you release more adrenaline, so the cycle of fear and panic escalates. Besides taking medication to control my mitral valve prolapse, I've also learned a technique that helps me control the inner fear that causes the panic to escalate. When I start to feel the effects of stress on my body, when I'm starting to feel short of breath (which I still do now and then), or if I feel a sense of gripping fear, I talk myself through what is happening. I know what symptoms act as a trigger for the downward spiral of the panic attack. I relax my body instead of stiffening it. I remind myself that a panic attack is stress-related. I know that to get upset about it is not going to help; it is only going to release more adrenaline into my system and advance my sensations of panic.

3. Panic attacks often cause people to fear that they are dying. When I feel a panic attack coming on, I admit this fear of death to God, and then I surrender. I say something like, "Lord, if you're going to take me, you're going to take me. I guess there's not much I can do about it." By surrendering myself to God and facing my fear, I can relax and quit feeding adrenaline into my body.

Even last night, I was keyed up because I was working on this book. My heart started to go crazy. Even though I could identify what was stressing my system, I thought it was over for me. I started to have mild chest pains and shortness of breath that could have easily escalated to a full-blown panic attack, but I surrendered and said, "Well, God, if you're going to take me now, there's not a lot I can do about it." And I just lay back and consciously relaxed my body. Before I knew it, I fell asleep.

Once you have a few experiences like that and you realize that the cycle of panic can be de-escalated, it doesn't have the control and power over you it once did. Knowing you can control your panic attack can enable you to get through it the next time.

I realize it sounds crazy to say that you should simply accept that you may die, if that is what you fear. But honestly, that is what helps me, and others with panic attacks tell me the same thing. This makes sense in light of understanding that our physical symptoms are intertwined with the emotional, psychological, and even spiritual issues triggering the fear and panic.

4. Face your fear. Whenever fear is overwhelming, I would take that as a clear sign that something in your life needs attention. Don't kid yourself by saying that you don't have the energy to handle your fears. Believe me, not addressing the issues takes more energy than dealing with whatever may be stressing you out! Do whatever it takes to confront what you're afraid to face. God will help you face it.

Note how fear ruled me and controlled my life. I wasn't able to go to the grocery store; I couldn't drive a car. Agoraphobia, fear of going outside, often starts from having panic attacks. Agoraphobics try to avoid the situations and places where the panic occurred because sometimes all it takes to trigger another panic attack is to go there and start thinking about what happened before. Their hearts race, and the cycle begins again. So many people are trapped at home, cut off from a full life because of fear. But agoraphobia can be conquered. How you conquer your fears may be different from how I conquered mine, but I hope and pray you won't stop seeking help until you have faced your fears enough to be freed to live life fully again.

5. Get a complete checkup from a medical doctor. Overcoming a panic disorder is not just a matter of talking to yourself or memorizing the right spiritual formula. If you are dealing with a panic disorder, you need to get a complete diagnosis from someone who can consider your condition as a whole person: body, mind, and spirit. Emotional problems, panic disorders, and depression are complex problems that involve all parts of you.

I don't know why people insist on believing that the psychological part of us is separate from the physical. The psychological is affected by the physical and spiritual. We don't fully understand the brain. So people mark things off as psychological, as though a "psychological" problem has less validity than a physical problem. The human brain is a physical organ. Our feelings, emotions, and physical behavior, all of these are a matter of electronic responses and chemical balances within the brain. Why can't we accept that the brain can get sick just as a heart or a liver can? We get ulcers because of stress, and we accept those. We have medicine to deal with the ulcer but when it comes to the brain, people create an entirely new category. It's like, we can't touch this—it's mental! Well, I'm sorry; my mental state is partially a result of what is happening in a part of my body called the brain.

Depression is not something you dream up. It involves a lack of seratonin necessary to transmit the responses between the neurons in the brain. So don't just sit there and let someone tell you to pull yourself together; you may be physically incapable of pulling yourself together. Even if you're afraid of what you might find out, face that fear and get professional help to find out what is causing your problems and what can be done to help you.

The same people who wouldn't dare tell someone suffering from an ulcer to "snap out of it" will say that to someone who is suffering from depression. Why is there such shame associated with mental illness? No shame is associated with a heart attack, an ulcer, or anything else that's physical. Yet the fear of being labeled a mental case keeps many people from seeking help.

I know the stigma of mental illness; I've encountered it directly. Yet I am open about my struggles—so open that people come to me and say, "I'm shocked you would tell people that you have had mental problems." I dare to be open about it because I want to encourage others not to cower in fear of being labeled by someone who doesn't understand their condition.

Our latest counselor, Dr. Gary Oliver, told me to look at my symptoms of stress as a positive asset. He says, "Quit looking at it as if it's a negative, Janice. Think of it as an alarm to you to tell you when you're not living right. These symptoms tell you when you need attention, when your body needs attention, and when there needs to be a change within your life."

One of the greatest fears I had to face was the fear that I would go back down into depression again. Many women who have been through depression tell me they battle the same fear. Gary told me, "We need to deal with this and face the fear of not wanting to go down again. Look," Gary said to me, "you've changed too much. You will not go down that low again, but when you start having those symptoms, you need to pay attention."

One of the greatest things counseling did for me was to help me understand the patterns in my life that contributed to my exhaustion and depression—patterns of overcommitment, trying to do it all and be it all to all in need, patterns of too much work with too little rest. Now I know the warning signs that precede going down again, so I can stop the pattern as soon as I recognize it. For me, warning signs come in the form of heightened anxiety and irritability, physical tiredness, looming fears, and a lack of joy for no identifiable reason.

Dr. Oliver assured me, "When you realize something is getting out of balance in your life, you're not going to ignore it. You can recognize when a change needs to take place." That is exactly what I'm learning to do. This is done by facing my fears, not by running from them. In this way I am overcoming the fears that once held me in bondage.

I realize that some of you reading this are not dealing with depression or panic disorders yourself, but you care about someone who is. To you I say, take charge and get help for those who are too weak or disoriented to get help for themselves. Bring people into their lives who are going to help them. Even if they say they don't want or need it, do your best to help them get a thorough examination by a professional or team of professionals who can help. Have them talk to somebody else who has been there. And pray for them. God will help you get them the help they need if you continue to seek his guidance.

One last fear I had to face and deal with in order to reestablish freedom in my life—the fear of failure. At one time I felt like a rat in God's maze, as though I was running down one corridor after another, trying to get it right. But now I realize God won't zap me if I make a wrong turn.

God knows that I'm dealing with a whole bunch of deficits. When my mind failed and I couldn't keep running, I discovered a wonderful thing: God still loved me as much when I couldn't perform as he did when I performed brilliantly. I came to realize that I am destined to fail sometimes, but since I am seeking to love God, he isn't going to punish me every time I show my frailty or lack of understanding. He may take me through experiences that help me learn to understand, but he isn't relishing the thought of punishing me.

Satan puts a lie out there (that the church sometimes supports) that we are to look and act a certain way. And if we don't act that precise way, God is going to strike us down! This fear can only be perpetuated when we don't really know the nature of our heavenly Father and how he loves us. He loves us as his children. Sure, he lets us learn from our mistakes, but does any loving parent punish a child who is learning to walk every time she falls? No, of course not. The loving parent simply picks her up, encourages her, and sets her back on her feet to try again. I no longer see myself as running in God's maze. I see myself as his child who is trying her best to walk.

And that has set me free!

Twenty

Living with a Rich Mix of Reality

When we moved into our new home in Colorado, I decided to do something a little different with our interior decorating. In my other homes, I had followed the decorating trends set by my friends and family, always conscious of how people might react. This time I decided to decorate the way I wanted to decorate. I've always wanted to add black as an accent color to my primary color scheme of taupe, blue, and rose. So I chose patterned pillows with a black background, a shiny black table, and a black afghan draped over my rose-colored love seat.

When I told people what I planned to do, I received the occasional wary comment, "Oh, that's . . . different," or "Hmmm . . . don't you think black will make your home seem dark?" But I discovered something beautiful about mixing the dark with the light colors. My home does not seem darker; it only seems richer. The people who were wary have been surprised at how beautifully my plans turned out.

My home decor serves to illustrate what God has done in my life. He took the little girl whose mother painted the world in pastel shades of happiness and brought in the dark colors. I'm not afraid of the dark shades of life because I know that the One who is doing the decorating wants to bring out beauty in my life overall.

My decorating scheme is different, but I've been learning that different is okay. I can be myself, even if I feel different, and not assume that I'm wrong just because I don't agree with someone. God transformed me from a woman who lived her whole life trying to please everyone, trying not to make anyone angry, into a woman who now can make decisions on her own. I'm happy living this life that is different from what I expected because I am free to be myself and to accomplish what I believe God wants me to do.

Although I live in this rich mix of light and dark, I don't live in fear as I used to. I'm not afraid to make mistakes anymore, because mistakes are a part of life. When I look back on my life, I'm upset by the things I didn't do because I was afraid that I would fail. Now I teach my kids that mistakes are tools by which we learn. "Don't be afraid to try," I tell them. "So what if you make a mistake! You learn through the mistake. Don't refrain from doing something because you're afraid you'll fail." Now I'm free to try things and take risks because I've been through the worst that I could imagine and survived.

I don't think the old Jan would have dared to write this book, for fear that it would not be good enough. When you do a book, you're guaranteed not to please some people. So it does take courage; but now I'm free to risk not pleasing everyone in an effort to encourage those who will identify with my story. That is a great gift. God has used my failures to give me faith that he can somehow use what I understand today, even though I realize that ten years from now I'll understand even more. This kind of acceptance of my own and other's humanity gives me freedom and joy.

Sometimes I think, *Who am I to be sharing my life story? I haven't arrived; I'm still in the middle of my journey!* But I have learned so much over the last five years of my life that I would never change the path the Lord took me on. The suffering—being brought to the end of myself—is what prepared me to comfort others.

How many people get to the end of their lives and say, "I wish I would have done things differently?" Well, if we really accepted that we're all going to die, we *would* live life differently. I live differently because I have learned to number my days. I treasure life more because I have seen how fleeting it can be, how life itself is out of our control.

The Lord has changed my heart in other ways, too. So many weaknesses within me I thought were strengths. Oh, I gave lip service to saying that Jesus was my strength and my joy, but I didn't live it. I relied on myself. When the journey God took me on showed me this, I was shaken to my inner core; I was shown how weak I could become. When my mind felt like a rusty computer that I couldn't rely on, I realized how weak I was and how strong God was on my behalf. I realized that God could take care of me *without* me, and the world didn't rely on Jan Dravecky. That was both a revelation and a relief.

Whereas I once lived my life as a people-pleaser, I learned that God does not ask us to please others but to please him. I no longer jump at every opportunity, even opportunities to do useful service for God. Now I can say no and trust that God will find someone else to do what needs to be done.

I remember David Jeremiah, our pastor in El Cajon, California, saying to us, "When you say no to someone else, you are saying yes to your spouse and kids." I believe God wants me to devote myself to him first, then Dave, then my children. After those commitments, then comes the ministry and doing things that may bless others. That's the way it has to be for me to keep my sanity and be useful over time.

I don't claim to live out these beliefs with perfect balance, but I have improved. Whereas I used to stay up to finish my work regardless of how tired I was, I now make sure I'm in my bedroom by 9:00 P.M. Whereas I used to start my work once the kids went to bed, I now go to bed when they do. I've made it a rule of thumb that once I've cooked supper, my housework and ministry work is done for the day. Dave and I may watch a show or I may read a book, but by 10:00, the lights are out. Then I get up at 6:00 the next morning. My old habit of overwork has become a rare exception. I don't want to go back to the way I was, so I don't do the things that led to my collapse.

I have put boundaries in my social life, too. We used to have something on the calendar every hour of every day. Now, I have no problem saying, "I'm sorry I can't make it," even for social occasions that I know will be fun. But if we are too tired and the occasion would wipe us out, it is not worth the risk. We now do one social activity a week, other than attending a small group meeting we belong to. That's it! Sometimes we get overcommitted, and then Dave and I check with each other and make adjustments. This helps me live my life in a way that doesn't get out of control.

Now I love it when my house is quiet! Moving to Colorado was one way we changed our lives. Our house in Ohio was constant action, with all the neighborhood kids in my house. We often had up to ten kids in the house all at once, which I did enjoy to some extent, but our home was never peaceful. We welcomed family and friends always stopping by because people knew where we lived. We even had strangers stop and knock at our door, and we didn't want to be rude and ask them to leave. It was your typical suburban neighborhood where the neighbors are always outside. So we never had peace and quiet or time alone with our kids. Now we live in the country, and when we're home, we're together as a family without interruption. When family comes from Ohio to visit us, they say, "I can't believe how peaceful your home is."

As I've made new friends, I've let them know how precious my time with my family is by respecting theirs. If someone calls at an inconvenient time, I feel free to say that I can't talk. This sounds like such a simple thing, but I would never have risked hurting another's feelings before. Now I let others own their feelings and reactions, and I am simply honest about our family priorities.

What I worry about more now is that I've become too isolated. I needed to draw back from becoming overly involved with people, so for a while I completely isolated myself. Now I'm learning to build relationships that are healthy but still have honest boundaries.

I remember saying to my psychologist, "Where's the middle? I've lived over here at this extreme, doing anything anyone asked of me. Then I went to the opposite extreme, cutting everyone off so that I could heal." Now that I'm feeling better, I'm trying to find a balance. But I found it hard to start getting involved in people's lives again because I was afraid of becoming overly involved. I wondered if I would know where to draw the line, or if I would let life drain me again to the point where I might go back into depression.

I've learned, though, that I do know the line. When someone who is hurting comes to me, I used to think I was supposed to remove her pain. Now I realize that I'm not going to be able to take away the pain. The pain is part of the journey, and I can't remove it. My responsibility is to come alongside others and comfort them, not to solve their problems for them.

My priorities and healthy boundaries help me keep my life manageable. That's why I needed to identify boundaries, like bedtime, how many speaking engagements I can handle, and how many extracurricular activities my kids can become involved in. Of course, we have to leave an opening for the Spirit to lead. There may be occasions when you are truly led by God to stay up until 3:00 in the morning with a friend. This is why my relationship with God is so important. I need time for self-examination and reflection to see if the life I'm living is in keeping with a healthy life overall and with what the Holy Spirit is leading me to do.

My heart goes out to women who have to work forty hours a week. I'm drained by the time I go home from the office, and I'm working only twenty hours a week. What you have to say is, "How busy is busy enough?" Then take whatever steps you can to create a manageable schedule. That is going to require admitting your needs and asking for help. Although asking for help can be difficult, I hope other women can learn from my breakdown and do something before their lives crash in exhaustion.

Remember, God built into the week a rest day, a Sabbath. In the Ten Commandments, he orders us to rest from our work and worship him. If we don't take the breaks that God has ordained for us, we may be the ones to break down.

Like most controllers, I still struggle with worry, fearing that events will not turn out as I had planned. Whenever I find myself worrying, I don't condemn myself, but I do take note of what expectations I have that are being threatened by what is happening. Then I ask if it is my job to control that part of life. Usually it's not. So then I use my worries and fears as a reminder to acknowledge God's ultimate control over all aspects of my life.

I'd like to close with one of my favorite quotes from Fenelon, Letter 15. This one helps me release control of my life to God:

> Live in quiet peace, my dear young lady. Do not have any thoughts for the future. For only God knows if you have a future in this world or not. In fact, you do not even have a today that you can call your own. A Christian must live out the hours of today in accord with the plans of God to whom the day truly belongs. Keep on with the good things that you are doing since you feel a leaning in these directions, and soon you will be able to get them done. But be careful of distractions and the desire to do too many things at once.
>
> Above all things, be faithful to the present moment. Do one thing at a time, and you will receive all the grace that you need.